The Freedom Letters

FINANCIAL FREEDOM
THE AMERICAN WAY

PROV 21:5

GENE HUTCHINS

THE FREEDOM LETTERS
FINANCIAL FREEDOM THE AMERICAN WAY
Copyright © 2011 by Gene Hutchins
Published by PCG Legacy
a division of Pilot Communications Group, Inc.

ISBN 978-1-936417-21-6

To reach the author:
4hutchins@verizon.net

To order:
www.pilotcomgroup.com/pcglegacy

PRELUDE

Stewards are chosen people. In New Testament times, the *Oikonomos*, or household manager — was probably better referred to as the steward. We even know some by name; such as Erastus, a New Testament times, biblically-referred to city manager. A woman is specifically named in Luke 8:1-3 as Chuza, the wife of Herod's chief steward. Well known movies, such as the epic "Ben Hur," depict Judah Ben Hur rescuing the Roman galley captain, and as a reward for his faithfulness he is given the man's signet ring of authority and named as an adopted son in his household with all the rights a son or steward would embrace.

Stewards were responsible for leading the efficient and effective management of the entire household; financial, assets, and investments. Over ¾ of the biblical parables deal with stewardship stories such as the wise steward, the unjust steward, and the steward who squandered the opportunity to invest his loaned talents. Obviously, the Lord found instruction and counsel on stewardship a priority; with the Bible citing over 2,300 verses dealing with money and possessions as they relate to eternity.

In *The Freedom Letters*, author Gene Hutchins uses vivid imagery and the context of an inner family tale to relate solid financial counsel. As a respected father and churchman who keenly understands the anticipatory duties of a deacon, Gene's appreciation for wise counsel in financial matters is a model for all who desire to live the life of a modern day *Oikonomos*. In trying and uncertain times like these, I found the financial truths he has woven into his story incredibly planful and proactive for those who seek out the treasures in each chapter of this book.

What I found most interesting was the way Gene uses the age-old tradition of fable and story-telling to relate crucial understanding of topics not familiar to many today; i.e.; compound interest for bad or good, debt, retirement planning, and insurance types and uses. Moreover, his keen sense of what to avoid is worth every minute of reading the story line.

Whether you are an emerging leader, college student, graduate student, newly married individual, or unfamiliar with the fascinating world of personal finance, author Hutchins herein relates complex ideas with ease that anyone can follow and understand. In fact, he has achieved what few do in a delivery method that is intriguing.

Stewardship is all about understanding who owns what and the responsibility we each have of service with what we have been entrusted. Gene Hutchins has captured what I like to refer to as inspiration for transformation. So many intend for the educational transformation of people with good financial education, but so often forget that it is inspiration that causes the change.

Bravo here to my close friend Gene Hutchins for successfully blending inspiration in story form to cause any reader a transformative experience. I hope you will reflect on your friends, ministry leader associates, and others that would so enjoy this good book. Then go buy a case load and bless those people with *The Freedom Letters*. You might just inspire a life or two along the way.

Scott Preissler, Ph.D., M.S., M.Ed.
Eklund Professor of Steward Leadership
Director: The National Center for Steward Leadership
Southwestern Baptist Theological Seminary
Fort Worth, Texas

FOREWORD

The American Dream...or is it? We made our way through high school and college believing the American Dream would someday be ours. Life, liberty, and the pursuit of happiness is ours for the taking as soon as we pay off those college loans. We have a wallet full of credit cards that we were never qualified for, and we step into the working world with little or no means for paying the debts we have accumulated.

Then we gain employment, earning a wage we are sure is below our real value and making decisions about spending that precludes saving for any future cause. Suddenly, we are entering the world of matrimony, mortgages, and maternity (preferably in that order) carrying our debts and flawed financial philosophies with us. Many older Americans reflect upon their 20's as one of the wealthiest times in their lives. Why? It's not because of the amount of money we made. Our 20's represented a time in our lives when we were less burdened financially and, therefore, more affluent. You see, it turns out that wealth is not defined solely by the money we make but by the money we keep. The sooner we learn that lesson, the greater our opportunity for real affluence.

This book teaches what every school in America should have taught us, but didn't. While geometry, biology, and theories of evolution were the required curriculum for many of us in school, noticeably absent were courses on the things in life that really matter — *things like financial freedom* — how to acquire it, how to keep it, and how to expand it. It is because of the absence of financial education in our schools that this book should make its way into every library. You will be hard pressed to find a course anywhere that will deliver the salient wisdom contained in this short read.

Gene Hutchins (a.k.a., Hancock) has drawn some excellent conclusions about what is really important in life while taking us on an adventure around our great nation to remind us of the price that was paid by many for our ability to pursue prosperity today. You may believe that prosperity comes only if you hit it big with some high-risk entrepreneurial dot com venture, but there is another way — follow the path Gene is suggesting and you will gain confidence in your ability to achieve the vision first imagined by our nation's founders and made possible for all of us by adhering to the sound financial principles shared in this book.

And while the fictional characters in this book are predominantly male, one should not conclude that this book charges only men with the responsibility for learning the lessons contained herein. Women, daughters, and granddaughters, you are granted no hall-pass. These principles apply to all of us.

As you digest the concepts shared in this book, consider the truth that you are not predestined for a life of financial scarcity. You can choose to take a different path. You can start with nothing, but you must get started. Procrastination is the silent killer of the freedom that can be yours.

Gene Hutchins imparts liberating financial advice in *The Freedom Letters*. My prayer for you is that you will be bold in your determination to achieve the steps to financial freedom Gene has made available for us.

Dawn Brinson-Roark
Founder — Brinson Benefits, Inc.

(Dawn Brinson-Roark is a young entrepreneur (44 as of this writing) who is the founder and owner of Brinson Benefits, Inc. located in Dallas, Texas. Dawn attributes her success to sound financial decisions made in her 20's. At the age of 29, with $40,000 in personal savings not counting retirement, she resigned from her corporate job to start a business which has evolved into a multi-million dollar operation today. Dawn's business venture would never have been possible without her determination to make sound financial decisions in the early years. While Dawn strongly believes that God is in charge of our harvest, she also believes that it is our individual duty to plant the seeds of our potential prosperity beginning at a very early age.)

PREFACE

There are any number of reasons why you have picked up this little book. Perhaps you're just thumbing through the pages to see if it can hold your interest while you vacation on your favorite cruise liner or you need something to help pass the time while you oil yourself next to the pool. In either case, consider the browse as time well spent...I hope. Maybe you want a simple guide on the process of wealth building. Nothing too complex, just basic instruction. You've come to the right place. I only do "simple" and "basic." In fact, my high school sweetheart and bride of 29 years says my writing constitutes "mindless entertainment." What exactly does that mean?

This book was written for the purpose of advising the next generation of Hutchins on what wealth in America is and how it's acquired. It is also an attempt to provide my children's children guidance on maintaining balance in one's life while building an American Dream. "Balance," as defined from a lifetime perspective of rewarding experiences would encompass the following: faith, family, friends, and freedom.

According to *Money* magazine, only seven percent of the American population has reached millionaire status.[1] In the land of opportunity, why is this number so low? Did our parents drop the ball? Did our churches? Or was it our education system? It concerns me that our high school and college institutions don't provide courses in personal finance. Maybe I should say they don't offer anything meaningful or of significant value. However, they do a great job of teaching our kids to be engineers, physicians, and scientists but can't seem to give them the basic tools needed to navigate down the financial freedom path. What's wrong with this picture?

I have spent the past few years studying personal finance and wealth in America. Through my study, I have examined more than 50 books and countless articles on the subject. From the assortment of canons that made up my study, this book was primarily inspired by four publications: *The Millionaire Next Door*, by Thomas J. Stanley and William D. Danko, *The Richest Man in Babylon*, by George S. Clason, *The Wealthy Barber*, by David Chilton, and *Financial Peace Revisited*, by Dave Ramsey. Three of the listed books are not necessarily laced with Christian values while one is. Nevertheless, I would recommend all of these manuals to anyone seeking meaningful instruction on personal finance. I need to add one more publication to the inspiration list: *The Book of Proverbs*. Without it, I would rapidly sink in the quicksand of life. A daily dose of Proverbs is what really makes a person "…healthy, wealthy, and wise."[2]

I am fully aware that anything a person wants to know about wealth and personal finance has already been written. Each book on the subject takes into account the author's personal preferences, spiritual condition, and/or political agenda. You just have to find one that suits you and yours. They all say about the same thing; however, each is packaged uniquely to satisfy a certain vein. It is for this very reason that I have written my own version of a personal finance guide.

Now I freely admit that I am no expert on the subject. I'm a public servant by vocation. I have no formal training on financial matters and don't intend to pursue any. The information contained in this manual comes from many years of trial and error, study, and massive quantities of divine intervention. If you need an author with a diploma of some kind hanging on the wall to justify the time spent reading, then you've come to the wrong place. I have no finely printed certificates or proof of advanced intelligence in the area of reaching financial independence. What I have is a lifetime of experience and many hours of reading and study.

Since my qualifications are so admirable (cough, cough) and the attempt to impress my readers with academic achievement isn't really working anyway, I deliver to you, *The Freedom Letters*. It is a very humbling experience to write a book; especially one on wealth and success. It's even more humbling to think that someone might actually read it! With all sarcasm aside, I hope you enjoy the story and find the information useful. I also hope it honors God.

Before you begin reading, please understand that this is an *opinion* book. All content and advice is debatable. You may agree with me or you may not. What has worked for me in the past may not work for you. That's okay. I can't say that I've always agreed with every concept or instruction I've read on the subject of financial freedom. I used what I liked and dismissed the rest. I'd recommend this approach to anyone beginning a comprehensive survey on wealth and success.

The target audience is primarily young adults beginning their first full-time job after completing their education. It really doesn't matter if you're a high school or college graduate. Once you've entered the American workforce, financial confusion officially begins. With any luck, this book will help you wade through the frustrating world of personal finance in a simple and didactic manner. It's also designed for those who've waited to address their financial situation. Maybe it'll help the late-comers find some stability before entering their retirement years.

Most of the chapters you're about to read include the following information: an interesting quote, several historical facts, a scripture or two, my opinion about the subject, and a challenging vocabulary word. To a simple person like me, challenging words are easy to find. Should you stumble across a word that you're not familiar with, you'll find a Glossary at the end of the book. I'm not really trying to stump you. It's simply an attempt to make the reading more interesting.

In the following pages you'll meet Deuce, Dolly, Hancock, and a chubby, old dachshund named Reggie. Deuce, a newly employed college graduate, is the grandson and protégé of Hancock. Dolly is the family matriarch and wife of the financial sage. Hancock is the counselor who unveils the map to the American Dream. As Dolly and Hancock tour the fruited plain, a pearl of economic wisdom is revealed at each stop. I wonder what they're up to…

— *Gene Hutchins*

ACKNOWLEDGMENTS

Completing a project like this cannot be accomplished without the efforts of many people. I began the manuscript thinking it would be a simple task that might take a few weeks to complete. What a silly thought. Several months later, I was still editing, rearranging, and compiling my thoughts. Help was needed. Friends to the rescue...

I want to thank several people who gave me wise counsel and encouragement along the way. Without the support of good friends and family, this book would have never made it to publication. The following people took time to read the draft, make suggestions, and afterward remained my friends. They recognized very early that I'm no Ernest Hemmingway. Friends are gifts from God and I owe all of you my heartfelt thanks. I value your friendship more than you know.

Boyne and Teri McHargue, Cheryll Duffie, Rob and Rhonda Branch, Robert and Jan Heineman, Ron and Kathi Hood, Skip and Dawn Roark, Art Wilson, Sean Manning, and Scott Preissler.

I also want to thank my two sons, Dan and Doug. You were the inspiration for the effort I put into the book. It is dedicated to you both...*and my future grandkids!!!*

A special thanks to my high school sweetheart, best friend, and wife for the past 29 years. Robin took the time to read, reread, edit, correct, and laugh with me as I stumbled through this thing. Her advice made the book much better. Robin, you are the best part of me...and I love you!

A final thanks to my Lord, Jesus Christ. You have blessed me much more than I deserve. You have shown me grace and mercy every day of my life. You overlooked my weaknesses, picked me up when I fell, forgave my sins, and kept me focused. You made all this possible, not me. Knowing You is my privilege.

CONTENTS

12   The Freedom Letters

CHAPTER 1

The Request

Dear Deuce,

Greetings from the four faces of Mount Rushmore! Presidents Washington, Jefferson, Roosevelt, and Lincoln wish you well as do Dolly and I. Did you know the four presidents that make up this monument represent the first 150 years of our country's history? These men were fearless defenders of the individual freedoms and liberties that we hold sacred. I hope we never lose sight of what so many have done for us.

As we approached the sculpted monument, I had to wonder why Teddy Roosevelt would be memorialized on a mountainside with the likes of Washington, Jefferson, and Lincoln. It seems to me that these three historical icons are in a league of their own. Nothing against President Roosevelt, but his accomplishments pale in comparison. Wouldn't someone like Benjamin Franklin or John Adams be more suitable members of the Rushmore team?

I did some research on Mount Rushmore and the reasons for including Roosevelt's profile are a little hazy. The artist responsible for the project was a man named John Gutzon Borglum. It appears that Mr. Borglum believed the American public perceived President Roosevelt in a mythological manner. He was a hero of the Spanish-American War, explorer, hunter, rancher, naturalist, and builder of the Panama Canal. Mr. Borglum believed Teddy Roosevelt embodied all the qualities Americans associate with a frontiersman who tamed the Wild West. He viewed Roosevelt's persona as legendary. For this reason, his image appears on the mountain's face. I still think Franklin or Adams would have been better choices, don't you?

I also discovered the name of the mountain comes from an attorney who was exploring the area in the late 1800's. Upon viewing the summit, Charles Rushmore asked a fellow climber in the expedition the name of the mountain. Bill Challis, a local resident and guide, replied, "It hasn't been named." From that point forward it was called Mount Rushmore. I'd prefer something more apropos like "President's Mountain" instead of Rushmore. In any case, this is a locale worth visiting.

Deuce, this is the first stop on the American tour we've been planning since Professor Dolly retired from Dallas Baptist University. Our intent is to visit the sites that make America great and pay homage to our heritage. Viewing these four faces of American history as the sun comes up brings out the loyal patriot in me. The Bible says, "...give thanks in all circumstances, for this is God's will for you in Christ Jesus."[1] We intend to express our thankfulness at each stop. We live in a great country.

Congratulations on your upcoming graduation!!! Dolly sends her love and says to tell you that we plan on being there. We can't believe you're really on the threshold of receiving your degree in business from Baylor University. What a great accomplishment! We are so excited for you and what the future holds. You have persevered and overcome many obstacles along the way. You should be proud of this milestone in your life. We are very proud of you and your success. Deuce, it seems like just yesterday that we were attending your T-ball games and watching you take swimming lessons. What a fine young man you've become.

We received your announcement in the mail just a few moments ago and have placed the date on the calendar. We'll be traveling southward to see the bluebonnets and Indian paintbrushes in blossom come April. The West Texas hill country always provides us a glimpse of God's handiwork. We'll make arrangements to stop in Waco for your commencement ceremony.

As I read the note you enclosed inside the invitation, you mention that you would like to develop a personal success plan. Your note says you'd accept any advice I may have on the subject. I am deeply honored and humbled that you would ask for my help. The "American Dream" is something few people in our country fully understand, much less ever experience for themselves. They don't realize you don't have to make a million dollars to be a millionaire. Instead, they waste their time and hard-earned money on things that have little value then wonder why they find themselves nearly bankrupt as they enter their retirement years. This is not what the American Dream is all about.

Deuce, my young grandson and graduate of the Baylor School of Business (can you tell I'm proud of your accomplishment?), I humbly accept your request for guidance on this matter. Each week from this point forward, I will send you a life lesson on various subjects that will help you create a personal plan for financial success. The path to financial freedom is long and narrow. Although it is an exciting road to follow, it is at times, confusing, frustrating, and disappointing. For the next several weeks, I'll look forward to our correspondence on building your own path to the American Dream. My prayer is that the information will be meaningful, useful, and honoring to the Lord who makes everything possible. You have my cell phone number and email address should you have any questions.

Although I'm no expert in any of the areas we'll examine, I am long on opinion and life experience. Any success that I may have obtained can be directly attributed to Divine Providence and the ability to get along with people. In fact, Teddy Roosevelt once said, "The most important single ingredient in the formula of success is knowing how to get along with people."[2] Deuce, this may be the first lesson in reaching financial freedom: *let God be in control and learn the art of human relations.*

As we proceed together, understand this: The guidance I pass on to you is information that worked for me and may not work for everyone. Please remember that any advice I give is only my two cents worth. I don't typically march to the pabulum of popular opinion. Therefore, use what you want and throw the rest away…

Your Loving Grandfather,
Hancock

CHAPTER 2

Plan

Dear Deuce,

Hello from the hills of Virginia. Dolly and I are standing inside the library of our third president, Thomas Jefferson. What an amazing place Monticello is! An architectural masterpiece, Monticello was the personal residence of one of our most brilliant Founding Fathers. Monticello is now a historic site that's open to the public most of the year. The gardens are carefully manicured and the décor is vintage American colony.

As we toured the complex, I was surprised at how little I knew about this American hero. Did you know that President Jefferson lived here for nearly 56 years, designed the home himself, and used only supplies manufactured from the property to build the home? The manor is located on a small mountainside which Jefferson aptly named "Monticello." Monticello is an Italian word that means "little mountain."

Jefferson's passion and vision regarding liberty and freedom laid the foundation for the America we enjoy today. His reputation after writing the Declaration of Independence and the conclusion of the American Revolution can be characterized as beloved international sage. His advice and counsel were often sought by kings and dignitaries. He was a highly respected hero to many around the world. Toward the end of his life, Monticello was filled with friends, family, and other patriots wishing him well.

Thomas Jefferson died on July 4, 1826, the fiftieth anniversary of the adoption of the Declaration of Independence by the American colonies. Ironically, his good friend and fellow President, John Adams, passed away the same day. These two men served our country well.

As promised last week, this is the first of many bits of guidance I'll offer in your quest for obtaining what most people can only imagine: The American Dream. Although financial freedom is not as difficult to achieve as many make it out to be, it ain't easy either. It requires a few foundational materials to make the goal come to fruition. The first and most important ingredient for success is to devise a plan. Most people who talk about financial success do just that...talk about it. Talk is cheap. Action is power. Benjamin Franklin said, "Well done is better than well said."[1] Don't wait. Don't procrastinate. Don't put it off. You must have a plan.

Careful planning is one of the cornerstones when building financial independence. It is vital to any successful venture. You've heard the familiar Benjamin Franklin maxim, "By failing to prepare, you are preparing to fail."[2] There is monumental wisdom in this statement. You can't get to where you want to go if you don't know how to get there. A plan is needed so get one in order.

You must define what your goal is, then map out a course of action. It is extremely important to put your plan in writing and place your written plan in a location where you can see it everyday. This will help you in the area of motivation. I know many well intentioned people who are great starters but never finish anything. At some point along the way, they lose their motivation. You don't want to fall into this trap. Don't put your plan in a drawer where you'll never see it or in a file cabinet where you may forget about it. A well written plan should not be held in abeyance. Keep it fresh in your mind. Read it everyday. Once you have a written plan and believe the goal is actually achievable, then, and only then, will you be ready to put your plan into action.

There are several important issues to keep in mind when you begin to write out your goal. Keep your plan simple. Simplicity is fundamental to any successful financial or personal goal. A complicated plan will be difficult to maintain and undermines the much needed willpower it takes to accomplish the task. Your will and determination are keys to accomplishment. Don't crush either with complexity. When I look back on several of my financial failures, I realize the root cause was the temptation to make my goals overly complex. I'm a simple man and simple is what works best for me.

Another issue to consider is time. According to Mr. Franklin, "Do not squander time for that is the stuff life is made of."[3] Unfortunately, we are all running out of it. From the moment we're born, the clock starts ticking. *Time is also what financial success is made of.* For the vast majority of us, there is no such thing as a get-rich-quick scheme. I've seen many of my friends spend several hundred dollars a month buying lottery tickets in hope of an unexpected windfall. If they'd just taken the money they spent on the lottery and placed it in a simple investment vehicle, they'd be relaxing on a sunny beach in Florida instead of rocking in a torn-up La-Z-Boy on the front porch. Proverbs 21:5 says, "Steady plodding brings prosperity, hasty speculation brings poverty."[4] Start early and allow plenty of time to reach your goal. Time is your most precious and limited resource. Use it wisely. I'll discuss the importance of time and how it affects investment growth in a future correspondence. It's an amazing and vital component for any financial independence plan.

You must also develop an attitude of consistency. You can't and won't reach any financial goal without having a consistent mindset. There will be times when you just don't feel like continuing with the goal or contributing to your own future. It's okay. I've been there myself. However, financial independence is only achieved by those who diligently hold the course. Your discipline to succeed will be challenged at different times along the way. Don't let complacency overcome the desire to be consistent in reaching your dream. You can do it, Deuce! You just have to keep at it.

Finally, don't be afraid to make adjustments to the plan as your circumstances change. I have, on occasion, tweaked my personal plan for success as the situation dictated. For example, when your dad was born, he came with a partner. Uncle Dean. Having twins was not in my game plan. The situation required aggressive action and somewhat altered my financial course. Two for the price of one is not a factual truth. Kids cost money. Dolly's decision to have a small litter of offspring at one time busted the budget. WHAT IN THE WORLD WAS SHE THINKING!!! (At this moment she's peering over my shoulder and laughing as I write these words. She keeps saying I was involved to some degree. My memory is a bit cloudy on the subject.) In any case, alterations to the financial plan were needed. Keep an open mind and remain flexible. Life happens.

Remember, my grandson, you must have a written plan to reach any financial goal. It's nearly impossible to be successful without a meaningful and simple plan. Use time to your advantage and leverage your cause with an attitude of consistency. Make adjustments when necessary but remain focused on the goal.

Lastly, lift your plan up to God and let him bless your effort. Jeremiah 29:11 says, "For I know the plans I have for you, declares the Lord, plans to prosper you and not to harm you, plans to give you hope and a future."[5] Isn't it good to know that God, himself, has a plan for your success? You just have to find out what it is and get on board. It may be wise to commit your plan to Divine Providence before the document is ever crafted. Let Him mould your plan into His. It's never too early to have God involved in the things that are most important to us.

Thomas Jefferson had the goal of building a special home for his family on property inherited from his father near Charlottesville, Virginia. He had a plan and put that plan into action. He aggressively pursued the dream one step at a time. You must do the same. Chart your course, commit the plan to God, and then make it happen. I look forward to seeing your "Monticello" become a reality.

Next stop: Philadelphia.

Your Loving Grandfather,
Hancock

CHAPTER 3

Income

Dear Deuce,

Dolly and I are standing in downtown Philadelphia, hometown of Benjamin Franklin, directly in front of the Liberty Bell. We're admiring the embossed inscription which reads: "Proclaim Liberty throughout all the Land unto all the Inhabitants thereof." The inscription comes directly from the Book of Leviticus, chapter 25, verse 10. I am constantly amazed at how God's hand has touched the American landscape in so many profound ways. Our tour guide stated the bell was last rung on George Washington's birthday, February 23, 1846. At that time, the crack on the side became so large that it ruined the tone of the bell's ring. It hasn't been rung since. Still, this piece of American history is a fascinating thing to view. Thank God for freedom and liberty.

Deuce, Benjamin Franklin is my favorite Founding Father for many reasons. His life story is a fascinating chronicle of rags to riches. Unlike the other heroes of the American Revolution, he did not receive his wealth by way of inheritance. Mr. Franklin became a printer by trade and leveraged his skills on the American frontier. He was a successful inventor, businessman, author, and statesman. He is possibly the first American to establish his fortune by way of work and perseverance. He made the most of his opportunities and became wealthy the American way. Hard work and determination made Franklin successful. His life story is the perfect example of how one can reach financial freedom. If he can do it, so can we. Like Franklin, one must grok the American Dream. Now on to more pressing matters.

I appreciate the kind note regarding the need to plan appropriately. Planning is something too many people overlook. It makes no sense to me that a person would have a meaningful aspiration but fail to plan for the goal. Hopefully, you'll pen the objective of financial independence in simple terms. A personalized mission statement will lay the foundation for a solid future. Keep it close and read it often.

You asked if I had a sample plan that you can use as a guide to craft your own road map to success. I'm going to show you one a close friend of mine placed on his refrigerator so he could read it every morning. This will give you something to work with:

> *To experience financial independence, I must acquire one million dollars. I can reach my goal if I save $325 each month at 8% interest compounded monthly for 40 years. This will produce: $1,053,586.26 not adjusted for inflation.*

As you can see, the plan is simple, easy to understand, personal, and something my friend committed to memory. Guess what? My friend is a millionaire...and he did it in half the time. In the weeks to come, I'll explain the process in detail.

The next step along the path to financial freedom is a little thing called "income." The importance of income cannot be overstated. You cannot build wealth without it. In fact, you cannot survive in any civilized society without it. If you try, you'll wind up under some bridge on cold, windy nights wondering how you got this way. In a country like ours, where opportunity is increasingly abundant, there's no reason for anyone to live below the poverty line. With your formal education and excellent communication skills, you shouldn't have to camp out under the stars or sleep at the local YMCA. However, you are always welcome to stay at the Mobile Marriott with Dolly and me. We have a spare bunk in the RV with your name on it. Come give it a try sometime...

Deuce, there are typically two ways to acquire income in a capitalist society: work for someone else or work for yourself. Most folks either work for a company or they ARE the company. Both have advantages and disadvantages. You have to decide which is best for you and your temperament. Let's take a look at both methods of obtaining income and see which avenue appeals to your mindset.

Working for someone else is the most common way to gather income in the USA. The majority of Americans, over 80 percent of our country's workforce, have a job that produces a wage of some kind. Gainful employment has a couple of advantages. The primary vantage points are *regular paychecks* and *benefits*. It's convenient to collect a paycheck each week, and employers typically offer a wide range of benefits for their employees. Another advantage is *mobility*. If you decide the job isn't quite right for you or your skill set, you have the option to seek employment elsewhere. You're not locked in to the place you work or the person you work for if something better comes along.

Once upon a time, I believed that *job security* was also an advantage but have reconsidered my convictions. Layoffs, downsizing, reorganizing, and reductions in force have me believing that job security doesn't really exist. Any company, regardless of size, can lose customers to the point of bankruptcy. Poor business decisions by owners or CEO's may result in having to spend the day at the unemployment office. Take a good book to read because you may be there awhile. Don't get all caught up trusting the idea that your job is secure. It's not.

I recently heard on a radio talk show that the typical American worker will be employed by *multiple* companies prior to reaching retirement age. Some of the job changes will be by choice. Some will not. Job security is all but extinct because of our rapidly changing economy and contracting out to foreign labor. Deuce, it is a good thing to hope for the best but plan for the worst. Job security just doesn't exist anymore.

There are a couple of reasons that working for someone else may not be the best avenue. The possibility of job loss for the reasons mentioned earlier can be stressful. If you're constantly worried about the next round of layoffs, then you may see this option as unworthy. Additionally, the length of time it takes to become financially secure as a company employee is usually substantial. Remember, time is your most limited but valuable resource. It will take many, many years of working for a company, or several companies, to obtain the assets needed to reach your goal unless you are an exceptionally high paid employee.

Of the two methods of gaining income we'll discuss, being an employee is by far the slowest method of acquiring wealth. Your employer is not necessarily interested in your financial well-being. The employer usually wants to acquire your skills at the lowest possible cost to the company. This means you will never be paid above what he wants to pay you unless you have extraordinary skills and can leverage those skills to your advantage. And even if you have an exceptional skill set, the price is still negotiable to the employer. The employer wants to hire employees at the cheapest price. Employees want more money. It's a constant point of conflict between the boss and worker. Climbing the company ladder and reaching financial freedom by working for someone else is usually a slow and cumbersome process. However, it is still possible and within reach. The key is creating and maintaining a positive income.

The next option for gaining income is to work for yourself by starting your own business. Self employment has a couple of advantages too. The two primary advantages are *control* and *freedom.*

Control of your business means you control your own destiny. You and you alone, have complete responsibility for acquiring income for yourself. It also means you can use your own creative capacity to develop your business as you see fit. You have to sell your products, skills, or services and charge a fee that is reasonable. If you don't sell, you'll starve. It's a pretty simple concept, isn't it? The marketplace will usually determine what that fee should be based on competition between you and other business owners.

Still, being your own boss can be very liberating as well as rewarding. You make all the decisions because you own the business. You are the "Chairman of the Board." Dolly's brother is the owner of a printing shop in Conway, Arkansas. His father and he built the enterprise from the ground up. Today, my brother-in-law is living very well because of his determination to succeed as a small business owner.

Freedom is what this country was founded on and nowhere is freedom more prevalent than in the small business arena. You, as the business owner, are free to choose your products, services, or vocation, and only you decide how much time to devote to the enterprise. The success of the business rests squarely on your shoulders. You can work as long and as hard as you see fit. Freedom is what lures many workers away from corporate America and into small businesses. Business owners are a unique breed of Americans. They're not afraid of risk and are willing to give their ideas a chance to succeed for the possibility of high reward. In a business owner's eyes, freedom rules.

As I just mentioned, the downside of working for yourself is risk. Risk of losing everything. Risk of a market collapse. Risk of losing customers. Risk of not earning enough to pay your bills. Risk of losing your health. Risk of making the wrong decisions. Risk of hiring the wrong employees. The list goes on. Still, working for yourself and owning your own business is an effective and efficient way to reach financial independence in a relatively short period of time. You must decide if the risk involved is worth the time. You must also decide if you have the intestinal fortitude to ride out the ebb and flow of owning your own company. It can be a very bumpy ride on the road to success.

In the book *The Millionaire Next Door* by Thomas J. Stanley and William D. Danko, the typical self-made millionaire in America is a small business owner. The authors state, "Interestingly, self-employed people make up less than 20 percent of the workers in America but account for two-thirds of the millionaires."[1] They also say, "About 80%...are first-generation affluent."[2] This means they built their wealth the old fashion way — they earned it. They didn't inherit their fortune from mommy and daddy like the Rockefellers or the Kennedys. They started their businesses, nurtured the business, watched it grow, made adjustments, and reaped the rewards for their efforts. Owning your own business is the quickest and surest way to enter Club Wealth. It ain't easy, but it works.

Deuce, the choice is yours. You've got to decide which way to go. Are you going to be an employer or an employee? The decision to own your own business or work for someone else is simply a matter of personal preference. One will usually achieve financial independence a little more quickly than the other but neither is certain. You make the call...but here's my recommendation. I believe a combination of both is the best option. Get yourself a good day job but don't rely on it exclusively. The possibility of job loss is too great. Some jobs last, others don't. Some companies grow, some don't. Pursue a small business in your spare time to see if you're cut out for the world of free enterprise. The only way you'll ever know is if you give it a try. The American economy is built on the backbone of small businesses. Our free market system typically rewards those who are willing to make the sacrifices necessary to achieve success in business. In any case, I believe the "combination" approach offers you the best opportunity for achieving the goal of financial independence in a reasonable time frame.

Deuce, I know I've given you a lot of food for thought. (Food? Hmmmm. I'm getting hungry. I wonder if Dolly would be interested in seafood tonight.) Just as the inscription on the bell reads, "Proclaim Liberty...," you can proclaim financial liberty by exercising the freedom to choose the path best suited for you. Whether you decide on employee, employer, or combination of both; remember, a consistent income is vital to building wealth successfully. Franklin once said, "Energy and persistence conquer all things."[3] If you remain focused on your goal and move forward with passion and persistence, you'll get there. There is nothing more liberating than crossing the threshold of financial freedom. Dream big, Deuce. Dream big.

Your Loving Grandfather,
Hancock

CHAPTER 4

The Gospel of Wealth

Dear Deuce,

This week Dolly and I are visiting the historic site of Gettysburg, Pennsylvania. This is a solemn place that serves as a reminder that we, as a nation, were at one time deeply divided. The American Civil War pitted brother against brother for the cause of freedom and liberty. The struggle between North and South resulted in the spilled blood of Americans whose convictions were polarized. I suspect the Founding Fathers foresaw the events of this war as our nation was being formed. Freedom for *ALL* is what the Declaration of Independence memorialized in 1776. Is it possible they knew what was to eventually unfold?

The Battle of Gettysburg was a watershed moment in the struggle between blue and gray. General Robert E. Lee of the Confederacy wanted war to be waged on Union territory. This battle was his attempt to move the theater of conflict from Virginia onto Federalist property. Had General Lee experienced success at Gettysburg, our country may have been called the Confederate States of America.

The onslaught began on July 1, 1863 and continued for three days. Lee's forces were repelled and began to retreat on July 4th. The battle was considered a victory for the Union army, but heavy casualties left northern forces weakened and strained. The total number of casualties and wounded for both armies exceeded 51,000.

Four months later, on November 19, 1863, President Abraham Lincoln traveled to Gettysburg to dedicate the battlefield as a military cemetery. The "Gettysburg Address" is composed of ten sentences and took President Lincoln approximately two minutes to deliver. Many in attendance felt the speech was unimpressive; however, it is now considered a masterpiece. This may have been Lincoln's finest moment. Deuce, of all the wars our nation has endured, this is the one that grieves me most. Let's pray we never see brother battling brother again.

I've been mulling over the proposed content of this lesson on wealth and happiness and I've decided to take the opportunity to offer a word of caution. "Wealth" and "happiness" are not always in perfect harmony. In fact, wealth can make a person miserable beyond measure if the heart isn't right and the mind isn't focused on the things of real value. If your goal is to acquire wealth for the sake of being rich, then I suspect your life may take an ugly turn for the worst. You see, my grandson, money tends to bring out the dark, underbelly of a person's character if priorities and principles for living aren't established first. The Bible says in I Timothy, chapter 6, verse 10, "For the love of money is a root of all kinds of evil..."[1] If a person has some hidden character flaws, money will not only expose the imperfections, it will amplify those flaws in dramatic fashion. Wealth isn't always good.

Take the character of "Scrooge" in Dickens's book *A Christmas Carol*. Here we have a man who spent a lifetime hoarding his money and ruining relationships along the way. He used underhanded and dishonest business practices to acquire his fortune and never once did he consider using his wealth for charitable causes. What a miserable, lonely, little man he became. I mention this story only to suggest that you lay down some steadfast principles of wealth now and promise yourself to never yield to the temptation to compromise those tenets. Let me offer a few that have made my life a little more peaceful, fulfilling, and meaningful.

I read an essay by Andrew Carnegie many years ago called "The Gospel of Wealth." Mr. Carnegie was the founder of the U.S. Steel Company in the early 1900's. He was a vastly successful businessman and possibly one of the wealthiest men in U.S. history. He states that wealthy people are trustees of their surplus wealth and should administer their riches for the public good. I would suggest you take this idea a step further. You and I are only stewards of the abundance of Christ and we have an obligation to God to use the things He gives us in a godly and charitable manner. We would have nothing of value if Christ didn't allow us to possess it in the first place.

With this in mind, establishing a few lifetime principles regarding wealth is in order. God should always be first in your life. The apostle Paul writes in the Book of Philippians, chapter 3, verse 10, "For my determined purpose is that I may know Him..."[2] Paul made a conscious decision to put God first in all he did and knowing Him his first priority.

Deuce, if you put God first in everything, you'll always have God on your side in all that you do. I can't think of a better reason for putting God first in your life. It has been my experience that when I genuinely put the concerns of God ahead of my own selfish desires, He tends to make good things happen for me. Usually when I least expect it, too. I don't fully understand it...but it happens. Having the Creator of all things working on my behalf has been a very comforting thought. Can you say "success?" God can and will transform your desires into His desires if you'll hold fast to the commitment of putting Him first in all you do.

Several years ago I read an autobiography by the great Chicago Bears running back Gale Sayers called, *I Am Third.* Mr. Sayers prioritized his life this way: "The Lord is first, my friends are second, and I am third."[3] This is a perfectly balanced set of priorities for establishing harmony with God and the people you care about most. You'll notice something unusually significant about this priority set: money and wealth don't appear in the top three.

Do you see the significance, Deuce? Earthly abundance falls to fourth place or beyond. It's not money or possessions that make for a purposeful and fulfilling life. It's that magical element called "relationships" that really matter. A happy and healthy life is made up of good friends and God. Gale Sayers has had a long and prosperous life making God his number one priority and nurturing his relationships. You can do the same with a similar outcome.

It is also important to recognize that money has no moral compass. It doesn't care how you make it and it doesn't care what you use it for. It has no conscience. It does, however, take on the moral direction and character of the person who possesses it. If you choose to make your fortune in an honest and upright manner and use your wealth for charitable causes, then your reputation in society will favorably rise. If you do the reverse, expect to be viewed with contempt…similar to Scrooge. In the Book of Proverbs, chapter 19, verse 1, God says, "Better be poor and honest than rich and dishonest."[4]

Deuce, I know this has been a lengthy and philosophical discourse on the subject of wealth. Stay with me because this is important. Preparing your mind to receive wealth is as consequential as the actions required to obtain wealth. Wealth can be either a healthy support blessed by God or a tool of Satan. It depends on how you prioritize your life.

Let's begin with a simple digest of worthy principles. You might want to consider committing to the following doctrines for honorable wealth acquisition:

1. Obtain wealth in an honest and fair manner.
2. Do not harm or cheat anyone.
3. Offer a fair price for goods and services.
4. Be known for quality, quantity, and service.
5. Use your wealth for good and charitable causes.
6. Give cheerfully to those who are less fortunate.
7. Honor God in all you do.

This list of fundamental precepts will work whether you're a business owner or under the employ of someone else. Make them your own personal gospel of wealth. Your conscience will be clear and you'll sleep peacefully. Creating wealth begins with the proper mindset. If you decide to adhere to this set of principles, you'll properly prepare your mind to accept wealth in a healthy, Christ-like manner. You'll also find the acquisition of wealth a little less stressful. In fact, you may even find that wealth gravitates toward you. Isn't that an interesting idea?

Let me leave you with this thought: The things that matter most in life are not the possessions we have or the size of our bank accounts. What matters most are the relationships we make and the people we care about. We should commit to love God and people, not money and possessions. Dolly says I should put Reggie, the attack dachshund in the love group too. Hmmm. Let me think about that...

Deuce, prepare your mind for the strategies about to unfold. Developing a healthy attitude about money and wealth will make the task of accomplishing financial independence an exhilarating and fulfilling experience. Keep your eyes open to what God will do if you'll just yield to His desires and make Christ your first priority. This'll be fun!

Your Loving Grandfather,
Hancock

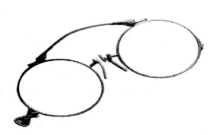

CHAPTER 5

Retirement

Dear Deuce,

Dolly and I have just returned from touring Mount Vernon, grand estate of President and Mrs. George Washington. What a magnificent little mansion it is. George and Martha charted their lives and our country's future from the manor located on the Potomac River. As we browsed each room, we could sense the love of the frontier and deep sense of patriotism they must have shared for the colonies.

We learned a few interesting facts about our first President that don't appear in most history books. Did you know that President Washington never wore a wig? It was his own hair that he pulled back and powdered. The story of the President adorning false teeth made of wood is pure fiction. Although he did wear dentures, they were not made of wood. His dentist fashioned his teeth using a combination of ivory, metal, springs, and an occasional cow's tooth. Ouch! That doesn't sound too comfortable to me. George never had any children of his own but he did help raise two of Martha's kids from a prior marriage.

After President Washington passed away in 1799, Mrs. Washington closed and locked their bedroom chamber. It was never used again while Martha was still living. She chose to retire in another room on the third floor of the estate. They were a great example for all Americans.

Deuce, I'm glad to hear that you're now a member of the gainfully employed. Congratulations, my grandson! The folks in the HR department of the Texas Medical Corporation made a wise choice by hiring you. I'm certain they recognized your excellent communications skills and superior aptitude for the position. Now that you have a regular income, building wealth in a progressive manner can officially begin. It all starts with your employer's benefit package. Let's make sure you have the right mix of retirement and insurance products to build wealth and protect your short term and long term needs. Some of the benefits will directly affect your climb into Club Wealth. Others will only protect you from unexpected loss. In any case, you'll want to sign up for those items that will support your goal of financial independence and ignore the ones that don't.

There are probably several benefits available to you. Some are necessary and some are not. The three that you need to invest a little time and research on are *retirement options, health insurance,* and *life insurance.* We'll examine each of these bene-fits over the next week or two. First item on the agenda: Retirement.

George Foreman, the charismatic heavy weight boxer once said, "The question isn't at what age I want to retire, it's at what income."[1] Deuce, I know you're probably thinking that you're much too young to worry about retirement. You may be thinking, "Right now I don't make enough money to save for retirement." Or you might say, "I'll start saving in a few years when my salary increases." My young grandson, don't let these thoughts impair your judgment. *Procrastination is the biggest detriment to reaching your financial goals.* If you'll begin to invest in your retirement account now, over time you'll find it isn't as difficult as you've imagined. In fact, you can fund your account automatically through payroll deduction. This is the easiest and best way to make regular contributions. You'll hardly even notice the pinch. Dolly and I did it for years while we were young. It's the reason we can travel the country and enjoy the evening sunsets. Our decision to automatically fund our retirement plans is now paying off. Big time!

Benjamin Franklin, my favorite Founding Father, once said, "Time is money."[2] You see, over time, *small money becomes big money.* Therefore, it's vital that you begin to invest now for the day you decide to stop working. Deuce, I can't begin to stress how critical this is. Funding your retirement account is the first and most important step to financial security. Remember, reaching the American Dream doesn't happen over night. It is a gradual process involving regular and consistent intervals of saving money. I'll illustrate in a future correspondence the affect time has on investment performance by way of compound interest. Keep this thought in mind, retirement funds are the cornerstone of long term investing.

Yesterday when we talked, you described in great detail the 401(k) plan you've been offered. *This is a gold mine in disguise.* I'll explain why in a moment. Let me first explain what a 401(k) retirement plan is.

What are 401(k) Retirement Plans? They are defined contribution plans the majority of employers at midsize or large companies typically offer their employees. They have become the most popular retirement option for most Americans. You have control over where your money is invested, and employers may contribute money to the plan on your behalf. This is what makes the plan such a great deal.

Deuce, *your* employer has committed to match your contributions dollar for dollar up to three percent of your pay. What this means in practical terms is the first three percent of your pay that you contribute to your own retirement fund, your employer will also contribute an additional three percent on your behalf.

That's free money! Don't turn it down! You can't make this kind of return on investment in any other venture! This is a no-brainer!

This is the gold mine I mentioned earlier. Your employer is making you an offer that you should never refuse. The only catch is that you have to make the first move. You have to sign up for the plan and contribute your portion first. Then the employer will match your donation. Deuce, don't let this get by you. It is a GREAT deal and for most Americans; it is the foundational spoke in the wheel of financial independence. Make a commitment to contribute AT LEAST the three percent of pay to the plan so you'll receive the maximum matching donation from your employer. If you contribute only two percent of pay to the plan, your employer will match only that two percent. That is throwing *free* money away. Don't do it!

I would also recommend you contribute something above the three percent matching threshold. Ten percent of your gross income would be a great start to the game of retirement investing. More if you can do it. If you really think that you can't afford the ten percent deduction each week from your paycheck, then contribute something, ANYTHING, above the three percent baseline. The more you sock away now, the quicker you'll see sandy beaches and palm trees. In any case, start now and don't put it off. You'll be glad you did. You'll understand why when you see for yourself the magic of compound interest. For now, just get started.

Where should you invest your funds? You mentioned the list of retirement options that you've been offered contain stock and bond mutual funds. Mutual funds are an excellent investment avenue for most retirement plans. Let me give you some basic facts on mutual fund investing.

Mutual Funds. There are two primary categories of mutual funds on the market: stock or bond funds. We'll only discuss stock mutual funds because stock funds have a great long-term track record and are the best option for retirement accounts. Within the two mutual fund categories are two types of mutual funds: *passively managed* and *actively managed funds*. Each type of mutual fund has a set of pros and cons that make them either advantageous or not. The primary difference between the two types is the use of a fund manager or group of advisers that select securities for a specific fund based on the investment objectives of that fund. The actively managed fund uses a fund manager, a passively managed fund does not. Let's look at both types a little more closely.

Passively Managed Stock Funds. These securities are also called index funds. Index stock funds invest in a market benchmark of holdings selected by a person or group of stock market observers. Examples of market benchmarks are the Dow Jones Industrial Average or the Standard & Poor's 500 stock indexes. There are several others that are useful besides the DJIA or S&P 500. I'm just picking these two for the purpose of example because they're fairly common investment indices. I'm not going to get into how each benchmark selects its own composition of stocks. Just know that these stocks are carefully examined or weighted in some way by the groups who manage their list. Why a stock appears in the index is really not important at this point.

As I mentioned earlier, passively managed funds (*index funds*) do not have a manager who researches specific stocks to see if they meet suitable investment criteria. These funds invest your money in the stocks of the market benchmark only. Since there is no research manager involved in index funds, the cost to invest in the fund is usually very low; much lower than an actively managed fund. Lower costs means you have more money to invest in the fund. This is a good thing.

Actively Managed Stock Funds. On the other hand, actively managed funds have a manager or team of advisors that try to beat the market indices by buying stock in companies that have certain growth potential. They carefully research companies to determine their value and potential for loss or gain. Most actively managed funds do not beat index funds on any consistent basis. Additionally, they are more expensive to own so you have less money to invest in the fund.

My advice: Small investors like you and me should stick with *index funds* only. We don't have the time or expertise to really evaluate the effectiveness of a fund manager or the stocks the manager is picking. Don't misunderstand, Deuce, there are some very good "actively managed funds" on the market. They are just not worth the cost nor do they consistently beat the market averages. Index funds are usually the best choice for small investors. Although index funds will only produce average market returns, the average is very good. Warren Buffett, one of America's most successful businessmen, once said, "Most investors, both institutional and individual, will find that the best way to own common stocks is through an index fund that charges minimal fees."[3] Mr. Buffett is one of the country's wealthiest citizens. He understands how to make money. When Buffett speaks, I listen.

Deuce, over the past thirty years the S&P 500 index stock fund has yielded more than eight percent total return on investment annually. Since inflation typically hovers in the two to six percent range each year, you'll beat inflation on a regular basis. Stick with index stock funds while you're young. My recommendation to someone as young as you would be to put 100 percent of your retirement contribution into index stock funds; simply because you have the benefit of time. The dollars you put in a retirement account should never be withdrawn until you actually retire. In fact, there are strict limitations on plan withdrawals and penalties if you do. For this reason, view your account as a long term investment only, and leave it alone.

Now if you've decided that index stock funds are the best option for someone as young as you, you'll need to decide which funds to put your hard-earned dollars into. Your employer will let you contribute a portion of your retirement dollars into one or more funds up to a maximum of three. This is good news for you because it lets you *diversify* your holdings. Diversity is a method of protecting yourself from poor performance. If one fund is doing poorly, you have two other funds that may do well enough to prop up the underperforming fund. Remember, all funds go through up and down performance cycles. However, over long periods of time, stock funds typically move upwards. Riding out the valleys of low performance is something that time can assuage. Don't get discouraged when you see a fund doing poorly for a short spell. This is normal for all funds. They usually bounce back pretty quickly.

Traditional 401(k) Tax Benefit. There is also an added benefit to investing in a traditional 401(k) retirement plan: *tax deferral.* Deferring taxes is another way of saying: putting payment off until a later date. Any money that you place in the fund is money that is not taxed at the end of the current year by Uncle Sam. This is a great way to reduce your income tax liability each year. Your gross income is reduced by the amount you contribute to the account so you only pay federal taxes on the net income after your contributions are deducted. We all like to lower our tax bill. The only catch is you must pay taxes on the contributions and earnings when you begin to withdraw the money. Uncle Sam says, "Pay me now or pay me later…but you will pay." We always have to pay the government in the form of federal taxes anyway. In this case, federal law requires taxation when withdrawals are received from traditional 401(k) plans.

Deuce, take a little time to review my thoughts on your company sponsored retirement options and let me know if you have any questions. I recommend index funds for the long haul and I'd pick three different funds for your retirement needs. The three that would probably serve your purpose are the S&P 500, International, and Small Capitalization Index funds. Ask your HR representative to divide all contributions equally among the three funds. Give these a try and reevaluate your decision in a few years. You'll want to give the funds plenty of time to track the market and see how they perform. If you have some doubts about your decision or you feel a fund isn't performing to your liking, you can transfer your holdings to other funds that are offered during your company's open season. You aren't trapped by your first choice of funds. In fact, you may want to occasionally tweak your retirement portfolio as your personal situation changes. Marriage, children, and promotions may impact your retirement perspective as your life evolves. That's okay. The main point is to get started now and start making regular deposits into your retirement account.

I'll end by saying this: Financial independence begins with investing in retirement accounts. The 401(k) plan we've been discussing is an excellent place to start. In a future discussion I'll describe the importance of investing in Individual Retirement Accounts (IRAs) as well. They're the perfect complement to the 401(k) and both are vital to securing your financial future.

Deuce, you're doing well my newly employed grandson. Don't be discouraged by the complexity of retirement accounts. We all have to wade through the regulations and paperwork, but it's worth it. Next week we'll talk about health and life insurance products. They're not real exciting but they're "MUSTS" when it comes to protecting your future. Hopefully your future holds something more than wooden teeth and powdered wigs. How about sandy beaches, palm trees, and fruit-flavored drinks with tiny umbrellas? I wonder what George and Martha would think about index funds? Do you think they ever spent any time on the beach? I just can't see it. Until then...

I remain, your loving grandfather,
Hancock

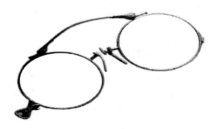

CHAPTER 6

Health Insurance

Dear Deuce,

Dolly and I are relaxing in the Mobile Marriott, reclining in our favorite easy chairs, and having a tall glass of iced tea after a busy day in our nation's capital. Washington D.C. is an amazing place to tour. The monuments that salute our country's founders and honor those who gave the ultimate sacrifice to preserve freedom have reminded me that liberty comes at a high price.

Our day started at Arlington National Cemetery and ended with a walk through the Smithsonian Institution. I guess I should say a walk through several of the museums that compose the Smithsonian. One day isn't quite enough time to see everything the place has to offer. It is the largest exhibition complex in the world with nineteen museums, nine research centers, and the national zoo.

I was surprised to learn the Smithsonian was founded by a man who was not an American. James Smithson of London bequeathed his financial assets to the United States for the purpose of creating an establishment to harbor knowledge and artifacts. The Smithsonian Institute, founded under the terms of his will, was thus created and continues to grow. What a great way to use the fortune he left behind. Mr. Smithson's altruistic heart berthed the gallery we now enjoy. We are truly blessed to live in America, Deuce.

By the way, Reggie the attack dachshund is feeling a bit under the weather tonight. The fat dog discovered an uneaten Snickers bar in the trash can and helped himself to an unhealthy dessert while his masters were gone for the day. I think he's beginning to regret the sneaky indulgence. When he looks up at me, his sad, sickly eyes appear to be begging for a bottle of Pepto Bismol. I don't think he got the message that yielding to one's appetite has consequences. Two minutes of ravenous bliss have resulted in a night of pure agony. If the chunky, little, low rider doesn't show improvement before the sun comes up, he might find himself visiting a local animal hospital. I'm sure he'll like that.

Deuce, as I read your letter, I'm encouraged to hear you've signed up for your company sponsored retirement plan. You intend to deposit ten percent of your pay among three different index funds. You say you'll make regular deposits to the plan using automatic deductions from your paycheck. This is great news, Deuce! Since you're contributing more than three percent of your pay to the plan, you'll also receive the three percent match from your employer. Congratulations, my wise young grandson! You've just taken a giant leap toward financial independence.

One more piece of advice on retirement investing and then on to other wealth matters. As you receive raises in salary, invest the additional money in your retirement plan. It'll be tough but worth it. Continue doing this until you reach the maximum contributions allowed. If you'll apply all increases in salary to the retirement plan, you can expect to see significant growth as time goes on. Remember, time and consistency are your best friends for building wealth. Benjamin Franklin said, "Lost time is never found again."[1] The earlier you start, the larger your fortune will become.

The next items on the list of company benefits that need immediate attention are health and life insurance products. These protective tools of wealth building play an important role in reaching financial independence. I'd call them "safety net" issues that safeguard you from unexpected loss. We'll look at health insurance today and discuss life insurance products next week.

Health insurance is one of those products that every person, especially those who work for a living or support a family, should not be without. One catastrophic event involving your health can devastate your financial well being. Time away from work due to an extended hospital visit or serious injury can be a very costly matter. Protecting yourself with a comprehensive health insurance policy will help you avoid a severe financial hardship.

Health insurance can be divided into four plan types: *Fee-For-Service (FFS)*, *Preferred Provider Organizations (PPO)*, *Point-Of-Service Organizations (POS)*, and *Health Maintenance Organizations (HMO)*. There is not a specific type that I consider better than the others. It just depends on your individual situation, need, or preference. Over the course of my work life, Deuce, I've tried them all. I don't really have a strong opinion about which one is best. I will, however, attempt to capsulate what each one provides and how it works so you can make an informed decision. Your employer may not offer all four health plan types. By law, companies are not required to offer them all. It's just great to know that your company has health benefits to offer.

Company sponsored health benefit plans are usually cheaper to buy than purchasing a policy on your own. The reason is twofold. First, whenever a company or several companies pool their resources and purchase a policy for their employees, premiums are usually much lower because of the high number of employees that are making premium payments. Of the employees that are insured, many are very healthy and rarely use their health benefits at all. The health benefits company can make a tidy little profit off of healthy folks and pass the savings on to everyone who's covered in the form of lower premiums. Second, your employer may pay a portion of the overall premium for you resulting in lower cost to you. You and the employer together, share the premium payment responsibility. This is a great benefit to have. Employers who value their people will usually provide some kind of premium assistance. Deuce, don't turn this down or waive your right to apply. Make sure you sign up for some type of health plan through your employer. It's usually a pretty good deal. Now let's look at each type.

Fee-For-Service Organizations (FFS) are also called Traditional Indemnity Plans. They work a lot like auto insurance. You pay a certain amount of your medical expenses up front in the form of a deductible and the insurance company covers the remaining balance of the bill or a portion of the balance. The typical FFS gives you complete autonomy over choice of doctors, hospitals, and other health care providers. Although you have the final say over who you see, you may still need to obtain authorization for certain services such as a visit to the emergency room. The downside of this type of health plan is it usually involves high out-of-pocket expenses before the insurance provider starts paying.

Premiums are usually a little higher with this type as well. Your deductible could be anywhere from $500 to $5000 before the provider begins to pay its share of the bill. Also depending on the terms of the plan, the provider may pay only 70 or 80 percent of reasonable and customary medical expenses. You get to absorb the cost of the remaining 20 or 30 percent. In a nutshell, a FFS plan offers flexibility and choice in exchange for higher out-of-pocket expenses, paperwork, and sometimes higher premiums. For some people, flexibility and choice are a high priority. If your employer requires that you do a significant amount of traveling, this may be the best option for you.

Reason: freedom to choose doctors and hospitals when you're away from home. Since Dolly and I are doing a lot of traveling these days, this type of health insurance option is what we've chosen.

The remaining three types of health insurance policies are called *Managed Care Plans*. Managed Care Plans have evolved over the past decade and are the choice of the majority of Americans. The goal of each plan is to reduce costs by requiring its members to comply with specific guidelines for service. For example: You may be required to use doctors, hospitals, or other health care providers that are members of the health plan network. You may also have to obtain approval from a primary care physician who is a member of the network prior to receiving treatment. The reason you would be required to use network providers for service is because costs are pre-negotiated at much lower rates with the providers. Since health care costs have risen dramatically over the past few years, managed care plan administrators have aggressively sought ways to reduce those costs. It's okay for a health care company to manage or reduce costs as long as coverage remains comprehensive. Cost reductions usually benefit you in the long run. Managed Care Plans have accomplished the goal of cost reduction with limited success. The following health plan types are all versions of managed care.

Preferred Provider Organizations (PPO) are plans that use the network system almost exclusively. You have incentives to use the health care providers in the network in the form of low co-pays for office visits, pharmaceuticals, or medical procedures. If you go outside the network, you typically pay a deductible for the procedure or much higher co-pays and the plan administrator may limit the amount they'll reimburse for services. This can be very expensive. Notice that flexibility and choice become seriously restricted in a PPO. You'll also spend time on the phone getting services arranged. If saving money is your goal, then using network providers only in a PPO helps you and the plan administrator. The downside of a PPO is administrative hassle and lack of choice.

Point-of-Service Organizations (POS) are plans that are similar to PPO's, but they introduce a gatekeeper or Primary Care Physician (PCP) into the mix. The PCP does all the service coordination for you. You must pick a PCP from the list of network providers, and that person becomes your first point of contact whenever you need medical services. POS plans also cover more preventative care services and may offer health improvement programs like workshops on nutrition and discounts at health clubs. Again, the down-side is the administration headache and limited choices for obtaining treatment.

Health Maintenance Organizations (HMO) are the most restrictive of the four plan types but are usually the cheapest. They typically require exclusive use of network providers. If you go outside the network, then you get to pick up the total bill. Although HMO's are not flexible, they are very inexpensive when compared to the other types of health care plans. They also have the best reputation for covering preventative care services and health improvement programs.

Recently, the health care industry has tried blending the basics types I just described. In an effort to further reduce costs, companies are being creative about services and benefits resulting in hybrids of health plans. Who knows what the future holds in health care? If the industry administrators can lower our premiums while maintaining comprehensive coverage, then I say give it a try. What have we got to lose?

If you have more than one health plan option, take a little time to review each one. Evaluate your personal situation and pick one that will provide what you consider to be comprehensive coverage at a reasonable premium rate. At this point in your life, you don't have the responsibility of a family so your premiums will probably be lower than those who do. I know that health insurance policies are confusing at times, but they are a great safety net should something catastrophic happen to you. It's time well invested and money well spent. If you have any questions about health insurance, just let me know and I'll attempt to clarify your issue. Well, maybe. It's confusing for me too.

Deuce, no matter which plan or plans your employer offers, you'd be wise to sign up for one. You need to protect yourself right away. Benjamin Franklin once said, "You may delay but time will not."[2] It's just a matter of time before you'll need the benefits provided by your health insurance plan. So don't put it off. Sign up for a health insurance plan quickly. Life and accidents happen. Both can be very expensive.

Next week we'll enter the wonderful world of life insurance. It ain't real entertaining but it's another one of the "must" items on the safety net list. We'll muddle through it together. I wonder if my health benefits will cover a sickly dachshund. Probably not...

Your Loving Grandfather,
Hancock

CHAPTER 7

Life Insurance

Dear Deuce,

Dolly and I have decided to spend a few extra days in Washington D.C. There is just so much to do and see, we could easily stay an extra month or two in our nation's capital and not get to experience everything. I'll tell you this, we are blessed to be American citizens and nowhere are this country's historical values on display more prevalently than the capital city. A spirit of patriotism is present on every corner. The men and women who brought our country into existence were light years ahead of their time. Their bravery in the face of radical opposition cost many their fortunes and their lives. I'm still humbled by the high price of liberty and freedom and thankful to those who wouldn't settle for anything less.

We had the pleasure of spending our day at the U.S. National Archives and Records Administration. Most of us know the National Archives as the keeper of the original Declaration of Independence, the Constitution, and the Bill of Rights. This morning we actually viewed Thomas Jefferson's masterpiece, the *Declaration of Independence*, preserved in a refrigerated display case. What a breathtaking document it is! Our tour guide said the parchment is beginning to degenerate due to age and the use of flash equipped cameras by tourists. Hoping to fetter the deterioration process, caretakers have now banned photography altogether. Their goal is to preserve the national treasure for generations to come.

The following statement in the declaration is probably the single most revered sentence in the English language: *"We hold these truths to be self-evident, that all men are created equal, that they are endowed by their Creator with certain unalienable Rights, that among these are Life, Liberty and the pursuit of Happiness...."* Can anyone really doubt this man was divinely inspired? Not me.

Deuce, as I read your letter tonight, I see you've signed up for a Health Maintenance Organization (HMO) type of health insurance plan. Taking the economic route to protecting yourself while you're single is a wise choice, my grandson. HMO's provide comprehensive coverage at a reasonable cost. I think you'll be happy with the benefits an HMO provides at this point in your young life.

Now what's next on the road to financial independence? Life insurance is something people hate to talk about but usually need. This item of personal protection is often misunderstood by the majority of people. Lack of understanding usually results in paying too much for products that aren't really needed. To fully understand life insurance, one must ask and answer the following three questions:

What is the purpose of life insurance?
Why do I need life insurance?
What type of life insurance should I buy?

Before I continue, let me pause for a moment, Deuce. I realize that you are not married and have no one depending on you for support other than yourself. Therefore, you need very little, if any, life insurance at all. Should you acquire significant debt prior to death then you may need a small policy to protect your parents and brother from having to account for the debt. Although this is not a legal matter, it may be a moral issue for your family.

You may also want a policy to cover the cost of funeral and burial fees so that relatives don't have to. Both are good reasons to buy a small life insurance policy though you may not need one. The advice that follows is offered should your situation change in the future. If you decide to marry and have a family then life insurance will become a priority. At that point, you'll need to have an understanding of what the product is and how it works. Here we go.

What is the purpose of life insurance? A life insurance policy protects your family from the financial obligations that accompany premature death. Unfortunately, death is an appointment we all must keep. We may not know the exact time but we do know it's just a matter of time. DOG GONE IT!

I believe it was Franklin who said, "In this world nothing can be said to be certain, except death and taxes."[1] Life insurance is preparation for what is certain.

Life insurance doesn't insure life so much as it protects those depending on you from losing the financial support that you provide. If you should unexpectedly pass away, your dependents would receive a sum of money to assist them with normal living expenses. Ideally, you will eventually acquire, through savings and investments, enough assets to provide this protection. For this reason, life insurance is not something you'll always need. Once you have your fortune in hand, kids grown, and no mortgage payments, you can stop buying life insurance. You won't need it anymore.

Why do I need life insurance? The simple answer is because you care about your family. Most people will earn between $1 million and $3 million during their lifetime. It is the loss of that earning potential that makes life insurance necessary. Life insurance is a substitute for the cash or wealth that would be accumulated by your family if the breadwinner were alive. Therefore, you're protecting them from loss of future wealth. The proceeds from a life insurance policy should support your family in your absence.

What type of life insurance should I buy? The array of life insurance products can be a bit confusing. You'll hear people talk about "whole" or "universal" life policies. You may even come across terms like "variable," "cash value," or "adjustable" life policies. These types are not wise investments for most Americans because they're expensive and rarely provide a reasonable return on investment. I'll explain why in just a moment. An inexpensive *term life insurance* policy will provide the best protection needed until you've reached financial independence.

Here's how a term policy works. Term life insurance is one that pays a flat amount upon your death if you pass away sometime within the contract term. For example, if you pay a monthly premium for a death benefit of $500,000 over a certain term; let's say 10, 15, 20, or 30 years, then your family will receive the face value of the policy upon your death. The payout amount will be remitted by check from the insurance company to the beneficiary, usually your spouse. It is insurance in its purest form. It is the best value for the money.

There are several items you won't get with a term policy. You will never receive interest on the premiums you pay. You will not receive any cash value along the way, nor do you have the option to borrow against the policy. Additionally, if you outlive the length of the term, your family will receive nothing upon your death. All the money you paid in premiums is now the property of the insurance company. You don't get it back.

Deuce, don't let any of this bother you. All of the items previously mentioned are high cost add-ons that provide no significant value. Insurance agents like these little options because they increase your premiums and the seller's commission checks. In my opinion, pure term life insurance is by far the best option for most Americans. Don't buy anything else or you'll be wasting your money.

There is also one big "NEVER" when buying life insurance. Here it is. *Never buy life insurance as an investment.* Life insurance is a product you buy to protect the people you care about should you pass away unexpectedly. *It is not an investment.* If someone tries to sell you a policy because of the "cash value" after so many years of making premium payments or they say you can get "market returns" on your investment, walk, NO RUN, as fast as you can. That salesperson is trying to take advantage of you and reap a nice, fat, hefty commission off your lack of knowledge.

Although there may be a cash value or nominal return on your premium payments, the amount is tiny compared to what you can make on your money if invested elsewhere. The monthly or annual premium of a typical whole life, variable life, or cash value policy is probably twice the amount or more of a good term policy. Buy the inexpensive term policy and invest the difference in a low cost index mutual fund. You'll save yourself a bundle of money and make some at the same time. *Never, never, never* buy life insurance as an investment vehicle.

Now that we have the three life insurance questions answered, let's talk about how much coverage you really need. As I mentioned earlier, an unmarried person without debt can probably do without any life insurance. No debt and no dependants means no life insurance needed. However, a young married person with small children and a mortgage is in a much different situation. I suspect you'll find yourself in this circumstance before too long. There are many "Rules of Thumb" when buying adequate life insurance coverage. Your insurance broker will want to discuss your situation at length so that he can offer you a product that meets your needs. My own personal rule of thumb is this: buy eight times your gross income while your children are young. Once they're out of college and your mortgage is paid off, reduce the amount of coverage to an amount that you think will adequately cover your own burial expenses. You don't need anything more.

At this point, the subject of life insurance for other family members should be addressed. A policy for a spouse is advisable under certain conditions. If you rely on your spouse's income or your spouse is the primary caretaker of your children, then a policy is recommended. If neither of the two conditions exists, don't buy a spousal policy. I also believe that a life insurance policy for children isn't really needed. The money is better spent in an investment account. We'll discuss investments in a future correspondence.

Now, the subject of "inheritance" is a debatable issue in terms of life insurance. If you feel a cash gift to those left behind after your death is sending the family a message of care or love, then by all means continue servicing the term policy. However, your goal in the life insurance arena should be to become self-insured by age 65 or sooner. Life insurance protects your family until you've had time to build financial security. Any inheritance typically comes from assets you've already acquired, not from a life insurance policy. Still, this is a personal decision that only you can make.

One final thought on term life insurance policies. Many policies that are called "term" are really not term as I've defined it. They may have an automatic increase of premium built into the contract. The premium will rise every five years or so. The insurance company will call it a "term" policy but don't buy it. Increasing term policies are only good for the insurance company, not you. Tell your agent you want a *level premium* for the life of the policy. This is always a better deal. I'd recommend a 20 to 30 year term policy on the family breadwinner who's less than 40 years of age.

Let me take a moment now to summarize my thoughts for you:

1. Life insurance is a product that protects your family from loss of future wealth.

2. Never buy life insurance as an investment product.

3. Only buy low cost term life insurance with a fixed premium.

4. Buy enough coverage to adequately protect your family.

5. Stop buying life insurance when you become financially secure.

Deuce, my young grandson, life insurance is one of those products that most people need yet never fully understand. As I said in a previous correspondence: hope for the best but plan for the worst. Purchasing life insurance is planning ahead for something you hope won't happen. If you adhere to the five items above, you'll buy only what you need at a reasonable cost. There's no reason to go broke buying something you don't really need. Unfortunately, many people will buy anything a guileful pitchman will sell them. Don't make this blunder yourself. If your employer offers a reasonable term policy, take a good look at it. See if it addresses your needs. Your employer might also pay a portion of the premium for you. It doesn't hurt to ask and it may be a good deal. In any case, let me know if you have other questions about life insurance.

As I said earlier, we plan to stay in D.C. a little longer. There's just so much history here I don't want to miss anything. The National Air and Space Museum on Independence Avenue is our next stop. Orville and Wilbur here we come...

Your Loving Grandfather,
Hancock

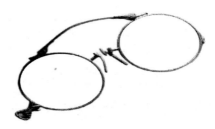

CHAPTER 8

Emergency Fund

Dear Deuce,

As Dolly and I relax on the banks of the Potomac River, we're reflecting on an eventful day of sightseeing on Independence Avenue. Our morning began with a visit to the National Air and Space Museum for a short tour of the "Milestones of Flight Gallery." As you know, aviation is in my blood and the opportunity to see the actual aircraft that launched us into the age of air transportation was a moving experience.

Entering the building that now houses these timeless inventions, the airplane that made the first solo trip across the Atlantic Ocean in 1927 is proudly hung from the ceiling rafters. My eyes were fixed on Charles Lindbergh's aircraft for what seemed liked hours as we examined each element of aviation history. I overheard a historian say that Lindbergh named the airship "Spirit of St. Louis" to honor the people in Missouri who supported his cause. The flight from New York to Paris took just over 33 hours to complete. Mr. Lindbergh won a $25,000 prize offered by a New York hotel owner for successfully completing the trip. From that day forward, Charles Lindbergh was a worldwide hero.

As profound as the Spirit of St. Louis is, the exhibit that captivated my imagination for most of the morning was the aircraft that started it all: "The Flyer." Designed by Orville and Wilbur Wright, the aggrandized Flyer has been refurbished and looks like new. On December 17, 1903, the first motorized vehicle to transport a person in the air remained aloft for about 12 seconds. Aviation as we know it officially began near Kitty Hawk, North Carolina. I wish I could have been there to witness it all. My own career in aviation can be traced to this single event in American history. I am beholden to the men who mastered the zephyrs of Kitty Hawk.

Well Deuce, this afternoon Dolly and I decided to relocate to a different RV park near Alexandria, Virginia. We wanted a change of scenery because the park where we had been camped was a little too crowded. Sometimes a moment of peace and quiet has appeal.

As we departed Cherry Blossom National Park and merged on to Capital Beltway, I heard a strange noise coming from the Mobile Marriott's undercarriage. I immediately located a convenient RV repair garage in the area and carefully transported our ride to the shop. I was told after a short engine evaluation by the mechanic on duty that the water pump was in disrepair. Oh no! How long and how much? Answer: a three hour job costing $1,100. OUCH! I guess I'll have to dip into the *Hancock Emergency Fund* to cover the cost. This brings us to the final rung on the safety net ladder: Emergency Funds.

Deuce, there are many philosophical ideas regarding an emergency fund. I'm not sure one is any better than the other. The key is to understand the purpose of an emergency fund then ensure you maintain an adequate cash balance should a need arise. Let's define the phrase "Emergency Fund" and then we'll identify what constitutes an adequate cash balance.

An emergency fund is a small liquid account you set up to cover the cost of unexpected events. The definition I prefer is: *a cash cushion that protects against unforeseen problems or disasters.* Remember my favorite saying: hope for the best but plan for the worst. Unexpected mini-disasters can seriously impede financial progress. Better to plan ahead and not need it than not plan and wish you had.

Unfortunately, life throws a lot of curve balls our way. Usually when we least expect it. I remember getting hit with a curve ball in my high school championship game at Diamondback Park in Pine Bluff, Arkansas. It was pretty painful and I saw stars for a few days. If you get hit with an unexpected expense, it'll be painful to your financial independence plan and may take months to recover. By the way, the Mills High Comets defeated the Pine Bluff Wildcats, 8-2. I wonder if I still have my championship ring.

When I say "mini-disasters," I'm referring to unexpected circumstances such as a broken water pump on the car, a malfunctioning garage door opener, or a leaking hot water heater. These are unplanned events that not only intrude on your financial well-being, but your time as well. Remember, this fund is to get you through small problems only, not major disasters. If your house burns down or you have a major car accident, homeowner's and auto insurance are the safety nets you'll use, not your emergency fund. If you fall off the roof and have to stay in the hospital a few days, use your health insurance to cover the cost, not the emergency fund.

It's also important to understand that an emergency fund isn't a give and take account to cover spur of the moment wants. If you want to order a pizza during the football game on Sunday afternoon, *don't* tap the emergency fund to cover the cost. If you think you need a new pair of Reebok running shoes or those Oakley sunglasses you saw on the internet, *don't* tap the emergency fund. Your emergency fund is to remain earmarked for mini-disasters only. Not mini-cravings or wants. Until a person controls his desires, wealth will remain at bay.

Also, an emergency fund is not for the purpose of supporting events that you know will occur in the near future. The car will need an oil change and new tires at some point. Don't tap the emergency fund. The house will need a pest control service every few months. Don't tap the emergency fund. These are not emergencies. They are events that should be planned for in advance and supported with other funds such as a regular checking or savings account. An emergency fund is for "unexpected" emergencies only.

Now that we've defined what an emergency fund is and how it should be used, let's see if we can agree on what an adequate cash amount is for a properly funded account. I've heard many financial experts lay claim to what an adequate reserve should be and all have valid reasons for their beliefs. Some experts will tell you three to six months worth of monthly living expenses will cover any unexpected emergency. I don't disagree with their assessment. I've heard others say that one thousand dollars is all you need. Again, I don't disagree. It's a matter of personal preference and what you feel is adequate security.

My recommendation is a cash amount equal to two months worth of gross income. Two months of my gross income in a liquid account has always been enough to cover any unexpected disaster. Deuce, you'll have to decide what amount is right for you. I recently read an article out of Purdue University regarding family finances that revealed 77 percent of all families in the U.S. had less than two months of gross income in a checking or savings account.[1] What would they do if an unexpected emergency arose?

Let me now offer a word of caution. There are some experts that say a cash fund isn't necessary at all if you have a credit card with a sizeable credit limit. Here's where I get off the boat with *these* experts. A credit card should *never* be used to cover a mini-disaster. I'll discuss credit cards and their purpose in a future correspondence. If you use a credit card as a substitute for an emergency fund, you're playing with fire. It's too easy to use that card for other purchases which is where many people start their slide into significant debt. Credit cards are tools of temptation that lead to debt. Debt is a dark hole that's easy to fall in and difficult to climb out. Debt is the enemy of wealth. Never use a credit card to fund a mini-disaster.

I would also avoid using certificates of deposit (CD) as an emergency fund account. CD's lock up your money for short periods of time and the bank will impose a penalty if you withdraw the CD prior to the maturity date. That means a CD is not a liquid account. It's difficult to get your money if you need it and you may be charged an early withdrawal fee. Don't use CD's for an emergency fund or any other investment vehicle that penalizes for early withdrawal.

Once you've decided on an amount for the emergency fund, you'll need to have a place to park the cash. Successful author and speaker, Dave Ramsey, conveys in his book *Financial Peace Revisited* that an emergency fund should be established in a place where you can get your money quickly and easily. He states, "An example is a simple bank savings account or money market fund that has check writing capability."[2] These are perfect vehicles for an emergency fund. Just make sure the account is free and you earmark that account for emergencies only. Don't use your regular checking or savings accounts for an emergency fund. In fact, I recommend using an account at a completely different banking institution. This will help you avoid using the fund for non-emergency events.

If an institution attempts to charge a fee if your balance dips below a certain amount, consider looking for an account elsewhere. You really never know when you'll need your funds or how much you'll have to withdraw. You don't need to worry about unexpected fees when a mini-disaster strikes. You just need to be able to get to the cash quickly. Checking and money market accounts keep your cash liquid and available for use.

Let's recap the subject of emergency funds:

1. An emergency fund is an account used to protect from unexpected disasters.

2. An emergency fund is for small, unexpected events that cost money.

3. Resist the temptation to use the fund for anything other than an emergency.

4. Never use a credit card or bank CD to serve as your emergency fund.

5. A checking or money market account is a great place to park your cash.

Deuce, you have just completed the "Hancock Seminar on Safety Net Issues." Retirement plans, health insurance, life insurance, and emergency funds are all valuable products that must be established before any meaningful wealth building can occur. Once they're in place, financial freedom is at hand. I'll be interested to hear your plan to fund unexpected emergencies.

Well it looks like our mechanic has completed the repairs in record time. He's rolling out the Mobile Marriott at this very moment. Maybe Dolly and I can find a fine dining establishment nearby. I'm thinking a little prime rib is in my future. I seem to recall a restaurant in Rosslyn, Virginia called "The Orleans House" that specialized in prime rib. I wonder if it's still there...

Your Loving Grandfather,
Hancock

CHAPTER 9

Individual Retirement Accounts

Dear Deuce,

Greetings from New York City! Dolly and I received a call this week from some old friends who attended church with us in Grapevine, Texas. They're flying into the Big Apple for a business convention and asked us to meet them in Manhattan for a few days of fun. We couldn't resist the invitation and hopped a flight out of Reagan National Airport. We arrived at Kennedy International late yesterday afternoon, had dinner at a local deli, and then found a bed and breakfast near

Strawberry Fields in Central Park. Friends are gifts from God, Deuce. I hope I never take them for granted.

This morning we toured the sobering excavation of "Ground Zero" in lower Manhattan. The site encompasses 16 acres of prime industrial property that was once the home of the World Trade Center. On September 11, 2001 our country was brutally attacked by terrorist affiliated with the Al-Qaeda organization, an extreme militant anti-American junto. We watched in disbelief as two air carriers slammed into the twin towers causing the deaths of nearly 3000 of our countrymen. Today, the site has been cleared of all debris and plans are in place to build a structure that honors those who lost their lives and American freedom.

Deuce, when this act of war occurred, I was working as an air traffic control supervisor at the Fort Worth Air Route Traffic Control Center in north Texas. Within an hour of the attack, all flights in the National Airspace System were grounded by the FAA System Command Center. Our instructions were to prohibit any non-defense related aircraft from becoming airborne for fear of further attacks. For the next few weeks, the American military dominated the continental skies. Air travel as we know it would never be the same.

Our President at that time, George W. Bush, made this statement a short time after the tragedy, "We will not waver, we will not tire, we will not falter, we will not fail. Peace and freedom will prevail."[1] From that moment forward President Bush's unyielding determination to protect our country from senseless terrorism and punish those responsible for the blood-shed became the aphorism of his administration. I'm thankful for a President who had the resolve to act on behalf of those who lost their lives and the families they left behind. Thank God for leaders who stand up to terrorism and thank God for peace and freedom. President Bush will be remembered as one who took American security seriously.

Now let's move on to the next phase of reaching financial freedom. Your letter says you've established an emergency fund at the community credit union. You've decided to acquire funds in an interest bearing checking account equal to two months of gross income. You'll rest well knowing you've protected yourself from unexpected disasters that occasionally arise. However, it may take you a few weeks, or months, to fully fund the account. That's okay, Deuce. Building up the reserve may take a little time. Once your account is fully funded, you can then focus on the next piece of the freedom puzzle: Individual Retirement Accounts (IRA).

IRAs were borne out of federal law to encourage American citizens to save for their own retirement years. I sense our legislators don't have any confidence in the solvency of the Social Security System created during the Roosevelt administration. So, they decided to establish an avenue for income producing Americans to fund their own retirement accounts. The result was IRA legislation. By the way, I'm in agreement with those who think the Social Security System is on shaky ground. We should all take ownership of our futures and not rely on big-spending politicians to provide retirement benefits. They just don't have a good track record when it comes to responsible spending. I'm not saying Social Security will ever disband; however, I believe benefits will be significantly reduced by the time you retire.

An IRA is an excellent instrument for building wealth on a consistent basis. There are strict guidelines for establishing and funding these accounts and severe penalties for non-compliance. The government doesn't always make it easy to understand the rules of engagement but it's still one of the best tools of personal finance to come out of Washington D.C.

To understand the basics of what an IRA is and how it works, let's examine the definition of an IRA and the types of accounts available. An IRA is an account that an individual can establish for himself which permits contributions and earnings to accumulate either tax-free or tax-exempt. IRAs are not joint accounts. They are for *individuals only* who have earned income. The funds in an IRA are for the purpose of building capital to use during your retirement years. As mentioned earlier, there are strict guidelines on the amount one can contribute to the account each year, withdrawals, and earned income limits. IRA accounts can be established at a bank, savings and loan, credit union, mutual fund company, or brokerage. There are generally five types of IRAs available to taxpayers. They are:

1. Traditional
2. Roth
3. Simplified Employee Pension
4. Simple
5. Education

Each type has it own unique set of rules and requirements. Deuce, I will only discuss the first two types because they are the primary accounts used by the majority of Americans. The other three are specialized IRAs that are used to address unique situations. All are excellent instruments for building wealth and all are supported by federal law.

A "Traditional" IRA is the standard account that began the wave of retirement investing. This type of account allows an individual with earned income to contribute an amount up to a specified maximum each year. The current maximum amount established by the federal government is $5000 per year. The maximum has changed from time to time but generally moves higher every few years. The amount that you contribute each year is deductible from your income tax return up to certain limits. In other words, the amount you put in is "tax-deferred" until you begin making withdrawals. Additionally, all earnings from account investments are also tax-deferred until with-drawals are made. Income tax must be paid on all contributions and earnings when you begin making withdrawals on the account. The earliest age that you can begin making with-drawals is 59 1/2. This is an excellent way to lower your tax burden every year until you retire. The primary disadvantage of a traditional IRA is that you must begin making withdrawals once you reach the age of 70 1/2 and there are penalties for withdrawals prior to age 59 1/2.

A "*Roth*" IRA is similar to the traditional with a couple of exceptions. First, all contributions are taxed prior to making a deposit into the account. Therefore, you cannot deduct your contributions from your income tax return. However, the earnings that accumulate in the account are "tax-free." You never pay taxes on the earnings while they remain in the account or after they are withdrawn. The maximum contribution to a Roth IRA is identical to a traditional. There is not a mandatory withdrawal age for a Roth IRA so you can contribute as long as you have earned income. The primary advantage of a Roth IRA is there is no tax burden when withdrawals are made. You receive all contributions and earnings "tax-free." The primary disadvantage is you can't write-off contributions each year.

The information above is an abbreviated summary and provided to help explain the fundamental differences between Traditional and Roth IRA's. To further simplify the differences; *traditional IRAs are tax deductible and Roth IRAs are not tax deductible accounts.* There are other nuances for each type but this will get you started.

When selecting which type of IRA to fund, you must ask yourself this question: Do I want to pay taxes on the account before or after I begin making regular withdrawals? You can pay Uncle Sam now or pay him later. This may be an issue to discuss with a responsible tax accountant. Over the course of my income producing years, I have funded both types of accounts. My preference is the Roth IRA. The reason is the benefit of tax-free withdrawal. Since I've already paid taxes on the contributions to the Roth IRA before they were deposited, I don't have any tax liability as I make withdrawals. For this reason I believe a Roth IRA is a little more advantageous. Of course this is my opinion only. There may be circumstances when a traditional IRA may have the upper hand and there may be a financial planner somewhere who's sold out to the traditional IRA. I still think the Roth is generally the best option for most Americans.

Once you've decided on which type of IRA to fund, you must then decide how to invest your deposits. I have always used index mutual funds for all my IRA investments. Since this is a long term investment it would be wise to take advantage of stock market returns. Although we've discussed mutual funds in a past correspondence, I'll go into more detail next week. Investing in the stock market through index mutual funds is a great way for small investors like you and me to fund our retirement accounts. You can also invest in certificates of deposit, bond funds, and money market funds for your IRA account. You won't get a very high rate of return on your investment but the option is there. Stock market index funds are my preference for all retirement accounts.

Deuce, if you'll contribute the maximum amount allowed by law each year, $5000, you will have a significant head start on the goal of financial freedom. The more money you contribute now to an IRA, the more your account will grow through the magic of "compound interest." Compound interest is an amazing investment tool that uses time to your advantage. I will discuss the value of compound interest in vivid detail in the not-too-distant future. The point is this: start early and be consistent. Contribute the maximum amount allowed by law so time and compound interest can work on your behalf.

Let me summarize my advice on Individual Retirement Accounts:

1. IRAs are long term savings accounts that allow you to invest for the future.

2. A Roth IRA is generally more advantageous than a Traditional IRA.

3. Fund an IRA using index mutual funds.

4. Start early and contribute the maximum allowed by law.

5. Let time and compound interest grow the account.

Deuce, this is a simplified explanation of IRAs and how they work. I have personally seen how IRAs can make one financially secure. Any sound investment portfolio will begin with funding an IRA each year. I would not advise anyone to invest in any other wealth building venture prior to funding their IRA. It's that simple. Additionally, the tax laws governing retirement plans allow you to invest in a 401(k) retirement plan and an IRA simultaneously.

Interestingly, I read a recent article that stated the total amount invested in IRAs as of the year 2008 exceeded 732 billion dollars.[2] That tells me Americans are taking their retirement future in their own hands. Building wealth with IRAs is catching on.

Well my grandson, Dolly and I intend to have a little dinner with our close friends and see a Broadway show tonight. I expect we'll be up late getting caught up. I've never been to New York and look forward to spending a few extra days in the gateway to America. If you have any questions about IRAs, feel free to give me a call. I always enjoy hearing from you.

Your Loving Grandfather,
Hancock

CHAPTER 10

Investments

Dear Deuce,

Hello my young grandson! As you know, Dolly and I have spent the week in New York with our good friends from Grapevine. Today was our last chance to see what this great state has to offer, so we chose the Statue of Liberty and Ellis Island for the grand finale. Touring the Empire State has been a rewarding experience.

We began our day on Ellis Island before taking in the majestic view of New York harbor on top of Liberty's torch. The Ellis Island Immigration Museum is the center of immigration history for our country. We spent the morning looking over old photographs and hearing fascinating stories of people who made their way to the USA in hope of building a better life. This location is known as the gateway to America, the funnel through which thousands have become citizens. The stories we heard bear witness to the courage and determination that enables men and women to leave their homes and seek new opportunities in an unknown land. This is what the American Dream is all about, making your own way and not relying on anyone else to provide for your needs. When a person sees opportunity and moves toward the dream, rugged individualism magically appears. Rugged individualism is how our country grew to be the greatest country on earth.

Unfortunately, the passion of purpose demonstrated by the early American immigrants may be a thing of the past. It now appears that comfort, affluence, and weak mindedness have diminished the desire for some of our citizens to succeed. The famous American poet Henry David Thoreau said, "Most of the luxuries and many of the so-called comforts of life are not only not indispensable, but positive hindrances to the elevation of mankind."[1] The rugged individualism that brought on courageous immigration and the industrial revolution is being replaced with complacency. Is it possible that wealth and comfort have suppressed motivation and progress? Has the desire to succeed been numbed by affluence?

There are some who believe a wealthy country should support its citizens through social programs and government handouts. There are those who don't want to roll up their sleeves and build a successful life on their own. They'd prefer to let Uncle Sam redistribute wealth so those who don't want to work, don't have to. Why has the word "work" become such an abhorrent idea? Benjamin Franklin said, "Early to bed and early to rise, makes a man healthy, wealthy, and wise."[2] It's a pretty simple concept; work is where wealth begins. Work is good.

In the Book of Proverbs, chapter 14, verse 23, the Bible says, "Work brings profit; talk brings poverty!"[3] God obviously blesses and honors those who work. This is why the Hancock family doesn't rely on government assistance for anything. We provide for our own the old fashion way. We get our hands dirty. We work.

I know I'm preaching to the choir, Deuce. However, the thought of wealth redistribution by so-called compassionate bureaucrats brings out my contempt for the slothful...and the bureaucrats! The nanny state is the enemy of rugged individualism. The nanny state is not what America is all about. Our government officials would be wise to encourage a healthy work ethic among the citizenry and make government assistance the program of last resort. Okay, it's time to chill. I've reduced myself to political polemics. My venting is over. Now where was I? Oh yeah. The Statue of Liberty.

As we took the ferry to Liberty Island for our final stop, I was once again reminded that liberty and freedom are precious items. Patrick Henry's passionate plea to the Virginia Convention in 1775, "...give me liberty or give me death!"[4] convinced the House of Burgesses to send local troops in support of the American Revolution. Liberty is one of those indwelled desires that springs from the heart of our Creator. The Statue of Liberty is symbolic of that divinely inspired aspiration.

The statue stands about 152 feet high from base to torch. The inscription on the tablet reads, "July 4, 1776" in Roman numerals. The monument was a gift from France and accepted by President Grover Cleveland in 1886. President Cleveland made this statement upon accepting the French pillar, "We will not forget that liberty here made her home; nor shall her chosen altar be neglected."[5] I am thankful that America is the bastion of liberty and freedom. I am proud that America is the home of the Statue of Liberty.

Since "freedom" is our theme today, let's see what's next on the road to financial freedom. Now that you have your retirement investments addressed and a plan is in place to fund the emergency account, we can look at typical American investments. The most common investment vehicles that have made the patriots prosper are *stocks, bonds,* and *mutual funds,* **The Big Three**. These are the choice of millions of Americans and foreign investors, who desire meaningful returns on their hard earned dollars. Deuce, there are other avenues of acquiring wealth such as certificates of deposits, limited partnerships, savings bonds, real estate, hedge funds, options, gold, currency exchange and on and on and on. There are just too many choices to go into detail about all. Therefore, I'm going to focus on "The Big Three" for this discussion. You'll see that of the three, only one really makes sense for the common investor. Now, let's do a little defining before we ponder their use.

Stocks or stock certificates are pieces of paper that indicate ownership or partial ownership of a company or corporation. When you purchase stock, you are buying a small piece or *share* of that company. Stock is usually purchased through a stock broker who may be employed by an investment service or brokerage house. A broker is a middle-man who buys and sells investment securities on your behalf for a fee. In some instances, stock can be bought directly from the company you wish to own. However, using a stock broker for purchasing or selling company shares is the norm. The value of the stock will rise and fall with economic conditions, growth and earnings of the company, new product design, product marketing, rumors, leadership, etc. As you can see, any number of items can affect the value of a company's stock. Deuce, this is a simple definition of stocks. Anything more will be confusing.

Bonds are interest-bearing certificates of public or private indebtedness. That's a fancy way of saying an IOU for agreeing to fund some project. An example of a bond-funded project might be road construction for a city, a water purification system, or a historic museum. Several years ago the owner of the Dallas Cowboys obtained approval from the city of Arlington, Texas to fund the construction of Cowboy Stadium through municipal bonds. The Cowboys now play in one of the finest stadiums in the country.

Types of bonds include municipal, corporate, and government bonds. When you purchase a bond you are agreeing to help fund the project associated with that bond for a specific amount of time. In return for your capital, the bondholder agrees to pay you a certain amount of interest during the life of the bond. Bonds are usually purchased through brokers or government agencies. Similar to stocks, fees will accompany the purchase of any bond. The value of bonds are typically determined by markets that rely on a bond rating agency. Moody's and Standard & Poor's are the most commonly used rating agencies. The agency will scrutinize the bond for investable value then give it a rating based on their evaluation. If I go any further on this issue, we'll both end up scratching our heads in frustration. Let's move on...

Mutual funds or Mutual Fund Families are companies that invest the capital of many investors in securities that support a common objective. Here's how it works: you pool your money with thousands of other investors to buy shares in a mutual fund. The manager of the mutual fund will invest your money in securities that focus on the objective of the fund you selected. For example, if you want to invest in a fund that buys stock in gold mining companies, you could find a mutual fund with that objective. A mutual fund will typically invest in many companies that are appropriate to the objective of the fund by purchasing stock shares of those companies. You and the other investors then become shareholders of many different companies through the mutual fund.

For clarification, you and other investors pool your capital and buy shares of the mutual fund; the fund manager takes your money and buys shares of companies for you. You are all joint-owners of the fund. You are also joint-owners of the securities purchased by the fund manager. There are several different types of funds with various objectives that are available for purchase, such as stock, bond, money market, or government securities mutual funds. Let's stop here. Simple is good.

So, there you have it, Deuce, the basic definitions of stocks, bonds, and mutual funds. I'll state for the record that purchasing individual shares of stocks or individual bonds is not a wise investment for ordinary Americans like you and me. I say this because we don't have the expertise to determine if a company or bond project is a worthy investment. We don't have the training. We don't have the time to investigate the investment risk. Therefore, we must rely on other people to tell us the value of the product we're considering. We just don't have the knowledge or skills to make an informed decision about individual stocks and bonds. For me, this is not wise investing. The risk is too great. The risk of buying an individual stock is like spinning the roulette wheel in Las Vegas. I'm not big on gambling. You and I have as much chance of picking the next Microsoft stock as we do winning the lottery.

The best way for a small investor to purchase stocks or bonds is through mutual funds. Before I explain why, let me define the phrase "small investor." A small investor is one who has less than a half million dollars in investment capital. Let me further explain my point on this. If a person has their company pension plan maximized, their IRA fully funded, their emergency fund account at the predetermined limit and has less than a half million dollars left to invest in other securities, then that person is a "small investor." That person should purchase stocks and bonds through a mutual fund only and avoid buying individual stocks or bonds.

It's possible, Deuce, that a competent financial planner may disagree with my perspective on the small investor. Everyone has their own opinion. I'm okay with that. However, this is my opinion: Most Americans are small investors and should refrain from buying individual stocks and bonds.

Now that you know my opinion on mutual funds, let's look at a few benefits of the investment. You'll see that the advantages listed will also be disadvantages for purchasing individual stocks or bonds. Did that make sense? Here we go:

> 1. *Professional Management.* The fund manager, or management team, is trained to identify companies or securities that meet the objectives of the fund. You pay a fee for their services but usually the fee is small relative to the knowledge and expertise they bring to the fund. If you bought an individual stock or bond, you would be the so-called professional manager.

2. *Diversification.* Since hundreds or thousands of shareholders are "pooling" their resources in a mutual fund, the fund manager can easily diversify investments among the securities of several companies. By owning many different stocks and bonds, the mutual fund can reduce the impact of a poor performing security. Diversification is an effective tool for reducing investment risk. There is absolutely no diversification with a single stock or bond.

3. *Minimum Investment.* Most mutual funds require a minimum initial investment to open the account; usually $500 to $5000 depending on the company you choose. Once the account is established, you can buy additional shares for a nominal amount. Most mutual funds have share purchase minimums that range from $50 to $1,000. It may be difficult to buy a dozen shares of stock or a municipal bond outside a mutual fund for these prices. Typically, mutual funds are very cost effective.

4. *Ease of Investment.* Most mutual funds allow you to make automatic investments through your bank or payroll deduction. They also accept personal checks and sometimes they'll take a debit card over the phone. Mutual fund companies are making it easier to invest than ever before.

5. *Ease of Redemption.* Most mutual funds will allow you to redeem your shares during normal business hours. The fund administrator will either send you a check for the redemption amount or put the cash in an account of your choice within 3 to 7 business days. Liquidating a

municipal bond in that amount of time may prove impossible.

Deuce, there are many other advantages to mutual fund investing. For time-saving reasons, I'll forego the list. Just understand this: The best way for a small investor to buy stocks and bonds is through a mutual fund. A mutual fund allows you to minimize risk and cost while receiving stock and bond market returns on your investment. This is, *BY FAR*, the most convenient and cost effective way to invest in the stock and bond markets. I may have mentioned this before but it's worth repeating. Warren Buffet, one of America's wealthiest entrepreneurs said, "Most investors, both institutional and individual, will find that the best way to own common stocks is through an index fund that charges minimal fees."[6] When Buffet speaks, I listen.

A word of warning regarding the purchase of mutual funds: avoid funds that charge a *load*. A *load* is nothing more than a commission paid to the fund company or financial advisor. When choosing a mutual fund, stick with no-load index funds. There's no reason to waste money on unnecessary commissions.

One final thought on mutual funds. According to the Investment Company Institute, Americans have nearly 11 trillion dollars invested in the mutual fund industry as of August, 2010.[7] That's a significant chunk of change! It's obvious that mutual funds have become the investment vehicle of choice for millions of American wealth-builders. I, personally, have invested in mutual funds for many years and will continue to do so.

Well, my grandson, we've managed to move through a very important area of financial freedom. I hope your head isn't swirling too much. I know mine is. Though, at my level of advanced maturity, head-swirling is normal...as are body aches and memory loss. Let me know if the clouds of confusion regarding mutual funds have been removed. I'm here to help.

Dolly and I are planning to return to Washington D.C. late tonight. We'll take the redeye out of LaGuardia and make tomorrow a rest day. We may do a little more touring of the nation's capital before we return to Texas. I'll give you an update next week. I wonder if the attack dachshund has held the fort down in our absence. We'll see. Bless you, Deuce.

Your Loving Grandfather,
Hancock

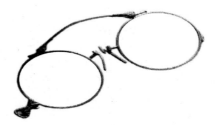

CHAPTER 11

Compound Interest

Dear Deuce,

Good morning my young grandson! Hope your day is going well. We are currently motoring down I-40 out of North Carolina en route to Texas. Traveling the eastern seaboard and absorbing the sites of American history has been time well spent. I wish we'd done this years ago. This great country of ours is rich in heritage and deeply influenced by the Creator of grace. We are truly blessed to live here.

Yesterday, Dolly and I stood in line for tickets to the Ford's Theatre National Historic Site in downtown Washington D.C. The tour includes the location where Abraham Lincoln was shot, Ford's Theatre, and the domicile across the street called the Petersen House, where he passed away the next morning. Ford's Theatre has a fascinating history. The building was constructed in 1833 and was initially a house of worship, First Baptist Church of Washington. In 1861, John T. Ford bought the church and renovated the building. The performing arts house he created was originally called "Ford's Athenaeum." A fire destroyed the building in 1862 which Ford rebuilt. The structure was reopened in 1863 and renamed Ford's Theatre. It had a seating capacity of 1700 and was considered one of the finest showcase structures of its time. Shortly after the assassination of President Lincoln, Mr. Ford attempted to reopen the theater but met public resistance. Upon receiving death threats, Mr. Ford sold the building to the federal government who used it as an office and warehouse.

Today, the theater is a fully functioning venue for plays and musicals. Although the auditorium has been remodeled and updated, the presidential suite has been carefully prepared and decorated in honor of President Lincoln. The President's seats inside box 7 overlooking the side of the stage are now retired and serve to commemorate our fallen Commander in Chief. The basement is a memorial museum where you can view the President's clothing and the Derringer used by his assassin. The Petersen House, where Lincoln died, has also been restored in vintage decor.

The death of Abraham Lincoln is a sobering reminder that leadership in a free society is not without risk. The desire to ensure that all American citizens, regardless of race, have the freedom to pursue life, liberty, and happiness was his passion. President Lincoln said, "As I would not be a slave, so I would not be a master."[1] Through the blood of heroes like Lincoln, liberty and freedom continues to thrive. We must remember that those who sacrificed it all are what make it possible for us to live as we do.

Before we see what's next along the path to the American Dream, let me answer the question your work associate has about mutual funds, specifically index funds. Last week I mentioned that Warren Buffet recommends index funds for most investors. I also recommend them. Your friend is right about guaranteeing "average" returns if you buy into an index mutual fund. So, what's wrong with that? The average is not a bad thing, Deuce. Over the past 30 years the average return on the stock market has been around 8 percent annually. I suppose the real problem is lack of excitement. For me, "excitement" is not a characteristic of strategic investing. It's a function of risk and ignorance. When it comes to investing, I prefer dull and boring with steady results over excitement every time.

As I said in a previous lesson, it's pretty unlikely that you or I will ever pick a stock that explodes in value like Microsoft. Searching for that one glamour stock is really a fool's game. It's like trying to find a needle in the haystack. I'm a firm believer in broad diversification. The more stocks you invest in through an index fund, the more likely it is that one or more of those stocks will perform well. This strategy is also a great way to curb your losses. I don't get caught up in the lure of instant success, Deuce. Like the Proverb says: "Steady plodding brings prosperity..."[2]

John Bogle, who's the founder and former CEO of the Vanguard Mutual Fund Group, is also the godfather of index fund investing. In his book *The Little Red Book of Common Sense Investing*, Mr. Bogle makes this statement about investing in index funds, "Don't look for the needle in the haystack. Just buy the haystack!"[3] Through the years, this advice has served me well. In the long run, a "buy and hold" strategy with index funds will usually lead to genuine wealth.

One final thought on investing in index funds then we'll move on. Most investors that attempt to beat the stock market end up losing their shirts. It's very rare that anyone can pick a group of stocks that will outperform the total stock market. Even the so-called experts have a tough time beating the market average on any consistent basis. So why risk it? I just happen to like the shirts I own and want to keep them. Let's move on.

The next item on the dance card of wealth is a fun little tool that many folks discover late in life. Sadly for them, time matters in the investment world. Dolly and I attended her high school reunion a few years ago and everyone was asked the following question: "What do you know now that you wish you knew back then?" A large number of her classmates gave the same answer: "the magic of compound interest."

Deuce, any meaningful plan to reach financial independence must begin with an understanding of *Compound Interest* and the *Rule of 72*. For the next few moments I'm going to pretend that I'm a brilliant math teacher. Well, maybe not so brilliant, but the results you're about to see will amaze you. Unfortunately, many of our academic institutions don't advise their students of this apposite information: Compound interest is vital for building significant wealth. Dolly's high school graduating class didn't know it. I'm sure there are others. I wonder why.

Webster's Dictionary defines *compound interest* as "interest computed on the sum of an original principal and accrued interest."[4] In simpler terms, it's the product of what you put into an account plus the interest you receive on your contributions multiplied over time. It is the affect of interest paid on top of interest received repeated over and over again. Your account grows by this compounding affect over time. Let me explain using numbers instead of words. This may help.

I went to a financial website this morning and found a compound interest calculator to use for the following example. You can try this little exercise in your spare time using a different set of numbers as well. Let's say a 25-year-old person has the goal of becoming a millionaire by age 65. Now, let's also assume the person has a regular income and can contribute monthly to the account for the next 40 years. If we assume that the average stock market return is 8 percent a year, which is what a good index mutual fund should produce, we have all the values needed to answer the following question: How much should a 25 year old investor save each month to become a millionaire by age 65?

ANSWER: $325 per month at 8% compounded monthly for 40 years = $1 million.

Although this does not account for inflation or any tax liability, it does show how time and compound interest works to your advantage. Deuce, I have one question for you: Can you save $325 a month for the next 40 years? Think about it.

Using the same numbers let's ask this question: How much should the 25 year old investor save to reach $2 million by age 65?

ANSWER: $625 per month at 8% compounded monthly for 40 years = $2 million.

This is called the magic of compound interest. Use any of the online calculators (the Yahoo webpage has an excellent tool) and adjust the numbers to see what formula works best for your timeline. If 40 years is too long, you can adjust the time limit for the calculation. Same is true for the interest rate. Some calculators have a marginal tax rate function as well. This allows for tax bracket adjustments. The numbers will amaze you.

Now that I have your attention, let me show you a chart that graphically demonstrates the value that time has on compound interest. Time is an important component of wealth. You can't waste it. The earlier you get started, the easier it is to acquire significant wealth. Take a serious look at this chart and ask yourself: "Can I afford to wait to start building wealth?"

STARTING AGE	ANNUAL INVESTMENT	ANNUAL RETURN	VALUE AT AT AGE 67
25	$8,000	8%	$2,433,948
30	$8,000	8%	$1,624,563
35	$8,000	8%	$1,073,708
40	$8,000	8%	$698,806
45	$8,000	8%	$443,654
50	$8,000	8%	$270,002
55	$8,000	8%	$151,817

As you can see, the earlier you start, the more compound interest works to your advantage. This simple chart changed my view about consistent investing...forever!

There's one more time and compound interest chart that I need to show you. This one illustrates why time and compound interest is the gateway to wealth. Carefully look at how Bob and Ed invested their assets. Each person contributed $2000 at the beginning of each year and received 12 percent annual interest.

Now I realize that 12 percent interest is a little unrealistic but it vividly illuminates the concept I hope to convey. All contributions and interest were reinvested every year. One started early in life. The other put it off a few years then began making annual deposits. Who was the smarter investor?

> **Bob** begins at age 19 and completely stops making contributions upon reaching age 27. He allows compound interest to work by itself after making only $16,000 in total contributions. Bob is a millionaire at age 58.

> **Ed** starts investing at age 27 and contributes $64,000 over the next 32 years. Ed doesn't acquire near the amount Bob has in his entire lifetime. He'll never catch Bob even though he continues to contribute every year!

Study the chart on the following page very closely, Deuce. A picture is worth a million dollars. It's well worth the time...

BOB'S INVESTMENT AT 12%			ED'S INVESTMENT AT 12%	
STARTING AGE	INVESTMENT	VALUE	INVESTMENT	VALUE
19	2,000	2,240	0	0
20	2,000	4,748	0	0
21	2,000	7,558	0	0
22	2,000	10,706	0	0
23	2,000	14,230	0	0
24	2,000	18,178	0	0
25	2,000	22,599	0	0
26	2,000	27,551	0	0
27	0	30,857	2,000	2,240
28	0	34,560	2,000	4,749
29	0	38,708	2,000	7,558
30	0	43,352	2,000	10,706
31	0	48,554	2,000	14,230
32	0	54,381	2,000	18,178
33	0	60,907	2,000	22,599
34	0	68,216	2,000	27,551
35	0	76,802	2,000	33,097
36	0	85,570	2,000	39,309
37	0	95,383	2,000	46,266
38	0	107,339	2,000	54,058
39	0	120,220	2,000	62,785
40	0	134,646	2,000	72,559
41	0	150,804	2,000	83,506
42	0	168,900	2,000	95,767
43	0	189,168	2,000	109,499
44	0	211,869	2,000	124,879
45	0	237,293	2,000	142,104
46	0	265,768	2,000	161,396
47	0	297,660	2,000	183,004
48	0	333,379	2,000	207,204
49	0	373,385	2,000	234,308
50	0	418,191	2,000	264,665
51	0	468,374	2,000	298,665
52	0	524,579	2,000	336,745
53	0	587,528	2,000	379,394
54	0	658,032	2,000	427,161
55	0	736,995	2,000	480,660
56	0	825,435	2,000	540,579
57	0	924,487	2,000	607,688
58	0	1,035,425	2,000	682,851[5]

What's important to see in this illustration is how Bob's $16,000 in *total* contributions grows to over $1 million because of the affect *time* has on interest earned. Bob doesn't have to deposit anything else! He let's compound interest do all the work and watches his account balance increase every year. Waiting a few years to start investing can be devastating to your financial independence plan. Don't wait Deuce. Start early. Bob is a financial genius!!

The other fundamental tool for financial planning is called the *Rule of 72*. It's nothing more than a simple calculation that determines when you'll double your money based on the affect of compound interest. Simply stated, your money will double at an exact point by dividing 72 by the percent of interest earned. For example: if you have $1000 in an account that earns 1% interest compounded annually, it will take you 72 years to acquire $2000 in your account (72 divided by 1% = 72 years.) Here's a chart that explains the concept a little better:

72 divided by 1% interest = 72 years to double your money.
72 divided by 3% interest = 24 years.
72 divided by 6% interest = 12 years.
72 divided by 9% interest = 8 years.
72 divided by 12% interest = 6 years.
72 divided by 15% interest = 4 years and 10 months.
72 divided by 18% interest = 4 years.

Pretty amazing, isn't it? Deuce, compound interest and the affect time has on your investment capital is where real wealth lies. The key is to start early and be consistent about your monthly deposits. Don't ever skip making a regular contribution to the account. If you do, you'll only be hurting your own financial future. *Time is wealth!*

Let me sum up this lesson with an easy exercise that will have REAL practical value. The maximum contribution per year the IRS allows you to contribute to an IRA is $5000. That's equal to $417 per month. If you put your IRA in an index mutual fund earning 8% interest compounded annually for 35 years and maximize your contributions each month ($417), you'll have approximately $1 million in the account at the end of 35 years. Since IRAs are long term investments anyway, is this a reasonable plan for creating wealth? This is not a subliminal message, Deuce. What should you do? Financial freedom is within reach. Don't go to your class reunion in a few years and wish you had taken advantage of compound interest!

Here's my recommendation. Read this letter again and ask yourself these two questions. Do you have to make a million dollars to be a millionaire? Is $417 a month too much to ask for a guaranteed future? Your IRA could make you a very wealthy man, Deuce, because compound interest is the gateway to financial security.

As always, my fine young financial apprentice, questions are welcome. Dolly and I are ready to spend a few days at home in Grapevine. There's really no place like home. Hopefully, the three of us can get together for dinner. How about Catfish Sam's? I'm looking forward to seeing you, Deuce!

Your Loving Grandfather,
Hancock

CHAPTER 12

Shelter

Dear Deuce,

It was great having dinner with you and your brother Friday night. Catfish Sam's Restaurant can put on a fine evening spread, can't they. My taste buds were craving a plate full of fried cuisine. Throw in a few hushpuppies, coleslaw, a little green tomato relish, a baked potato and watch the cholesterol count slowly rise. OH YEAH! There's just something special about a night of unhealthy gluttonous behavior with a couple of fellow Hancocks. You two sure know how to put away a short stack of fish fillets. Now, it's back to the low-fat diet so Dr. Williams doesn't put me on probation…again. Dog gone it!

Dolly and I spent Saturday afternoon with some old friends from college who dropped by on their way to the Grand Canyon. They wanted to see the John F. Kennedy Memorial so we made a special trip to Dealey Plaza. November 22, 1963 was not a good day in Dallas. As our country mourned the loss of an extraordinary man, the image of John Jr. saluting his father during the President's funeral remains an emotional memory. This heart-wrenching event serves as a serious reminder that leadership in a free society can have grave consequences.

The Dealey Plaza Historic District is now a nationally preserved area on the west side of Dallas. The site encompasses approximately 150 acres around the location where three streets converge: Main, Elm, and Commerce. The sixth and seventh floors of the old Texas School Book Depository building are the home of artifacts commemorating the life of our beloved president. The actual cenotaph to President Kennedy is located on Commerce Street. Why anyone would want to extinguish this man's life is beyond reason.

President Kennedy was well respected by the citizens of this country and foreigners alike. His presence offered hope and promise to our country after the devastation of World War II and the Korean conflict. The young leader's optimistic views on liberty and freedom paralleled those of Jefferson and Lincoln. President Kennedy's encouraging outlook on life and government can be seen in his own words, "We should not let our fears hold us back from pursuing our hopes."[1] The United States could use more leaders like JFK. I doubt America has ever fully recovered from the loss.

Well Deuce, after relaxing at home the past two weeks, Dolly and I are packing the RV for yet another short trip. Our destination: the left coast of California and beyond. Who knows where we might end up? Maybe Alaska or Hawaii? We'll see.

Before we hitch-up the mule team for the journey across the fruited plain, let's discuss what many say is the heart of Americanism: the house. Deuce, owning a home is what represents the idea we call "The American Dream." When you buy a house, you own a piece of America. Home ownership and property rights are integral pieces of life, liberty, and the pursuit of happiness. When someone reaches the point in their life where they can afford a house, a sense of accomplishment and success as an American citizen prevails. Pride of ownership is something that every American should experience at some point.

Home ownership has many benefits with a few pitfalls. Many say it is the best "investment" you'll ever make. Hmmmm. I'm not sure I'm in total agreement. The cost of owning a house is like putting a siphon hose on the savings account. I've often wondered: Do I own the house or does it own me? It can be an expensive proposition.

In fact, my views on owning a home run somewhat counter to the prevailing wisdom of the day. Submitting to vox populi is not for me. I have never bought a house that I reside in for "investment" purposes, Deuce. I view my home as a safe and secure place for my family to live, not so much an investment. However, I do believe that owning a home can be an opportunity for significant wealth creation. I'll explain why in a moment...

For this discussion I'll focus on homeownership as it pertains to a primary residence only and not rental property. The pros and cons of owning rental property will be reserved for a future conversation. When we return from our travels, let's discuss the subject at Starbuck's over a cup of Sumatra.

Although many will argue that homeownership is the cornerstone of American wealth, a primary residence should be viewed as shelter for you and your family. Most people have two choices when it comes to choosing shelter: rent or buy. In either case, where and what you rent (or buy) is an important decision.

Renting may have some advantages over buying, especially during downturns in the economy. When housing prices begin to fall, a renter doesn't have to deal with the emotional stress of losing money on the value of his property. If you view a house as an investment, it's either a good or bad investment depending on economic conditions. A friend of mine, who bought a condominium several years ago in Southern California, told me recently the value of his home was 25% less than the purchase price. OUCH! Was that a good investment?

Additionally, renters typically don't contend with mainte- nance issues. The cost to fix an appliance or leaking hot water heater is the responsibility of the owner, not the renter. Unless the renter is guilty of abuse, the owner must maintain the property. Things tend to break down and repairs can be costly.

Renting also allows for relocation flexibility. If your job requires you to move to a different city on a regular basis, selling a property isn't a concern. You are free to go. There may be an early lease termination fee, but that's usually minimal compared to the headache of selling property. You see, Deuce, renting does have a few advantages. You just have to evaluate your circumstances and decide for yourself. My personal rule of thumb has been to avoid buying a primary residence if it's likely I'll relocate within 5 years. If relocation is certain, renting would be my preference. However, purchasing a home may be the best option when long-term residency is expected.

I mentioned earlier that owning a house could be an avenue for creating exceptional wealth. It takes a unique set of circumstances to make your residence an opportunity for serious wealth building, but it is possible. I'll explain the process after we unveil a few facts about wealthy Americans.

Several years ago I read a fascinating book by Thomas J. Stanley and William D. Danko called *The Millionaire Next Door*. The authors state that 97% of millionaires in this country are homeowners.[2] That's a significant fact regarding wealth and says something about the necessity of homeownership as it relates to acquiring wealth. Wealthy people tend to own their homes. Additionally, of the millionaires that own their houses, nearly 50% have occupied their residence for 20 years or more.[3] You see, Deuce, wealthy folks prefer to buy and hold their primary residence. They don't jump from house to house every few years. They let their equity build up gradually over time at the same location. Isn't it interesting that affluent Americans typically remain in their homes for long periods of time? One of our country's wealthiest businessmen, Warren Buffet, still occupies the home he bought in 1958.

The concept of buying a house and staying in the same location for many years runs counter to what is common practice today. There are financial experts who will advise their clients to do silly things and make it sound like shrewd investing. Here are a few fallacious ideas regarding the purchase of a home:

> *1. Buy as much house as you can finance. Any future raises received will make your monthly payments easier to afford as time goes by.*

> *2. Use a 30-year mortgage to pay for the house. Leveraging other people's money is how wealth is built.*

> *3. Sell your home and buy a bigger, more expensive house every few years. Homes normally go up in value so you'll make money on your transactions.*

Deuce, this is not wise investment strategy and may actually squelch your plan for meaningful wealth building. Although the advice isn't necessarily false, it isn't always true. Debt has become a catastrophic problem for many Americans. Since buying a house is normally our largest expense, careful planning and serious thought should accompany the purchase.

I have always approached financial independence from a perspective that's contrary to many in the asset acquisition profession. My views will often conflict with common investment practices. Deuce, I'm now going to address each of the three items above individually. Remember, this is my opinion only, and the advice I offer comes with experience. What I'm about to say, I've also done.

The phrase "buy as much house as you can finance" has this meaning: stretch your budget to the limit. Why would anyone want to spread their available resources thin? Do you want to eat macaroni and cheese for dinner every night? Of course not. So don't do it. A mortgage lender will typically say that an applicant for a home loan can afford payments equal to 25 to 40 percent of their monthly gross income. That's a sizeable chunk of change. I've never bought a house for the purpose of impressing my friends or work associates. Owning a "trophy home" just hasn't been a high priority for me. My habit has been to buy a modest house in a good, safe, middle-class neighborhood for about half what a lender says I can afford. Although I don't suggest a "trophy home," I will recommend the purchase of a quality home by a reputable builder. I also believe the owner should update and renovate periodically. Beautifying and maintaining your residence adds value and provides peace of mind. Your home represents you and should reflect your standards. It is a valuable asset that you should care for. Treat it wisely.

Deuce, I've never understood the idea that future raises will always make your house payment easier. At best, the premise is weak. If your family grows, so will living expenses. Inflation may also absorb your raise or bonus. And what if the unthinkable happens; your employer doesn't give you a raise or bonus? It makes no sense to me that anyone would rely on using money they don't have. There are no guarantees. Life has enough tribulation without adding the stress of ultra-high mortgage payments. Remember, hope for the best but plan for the worst.

Although there may be valid reasons for obtaining a 30-year mortgage, I rarely, if ever, recommend one. I have many reasons for my somewhat extreme position on this matter. Here are a few. Over time (30 years,) you would pay the lending company more in interest payments than the purchase price of the house. Do you want to make a mortgage banker wealthy? Of course not. So don't do it. I understand the argument of "leveraging" other people's money and not your own. However, it's still debt that has to be paid. If you plan on living in the home for an extended period of time, why pay the mortgage company extra interest when it isn't necessary? A 15-year mortgage could save you thousands of dollars in interest compared to a 30-year loan. Additionally, the monthly payment on a 15-year loan isn't much more than a 30-year note. You also build equity at a much faster rate with a 15-year loan.

Let me explain my thoughts in graphic detail. The following scenario illustrates the difference between a 30-year and 15-year mortgage. If you buy a $100,000 dollar house, put 20%

down and finance the remaining $80,000 dollars at 10% interest, your payments would be as follows:

"30 years OR 360 payments at $702 per month equals $252,720 total.

15 years OR 180 payments at $860 per month equals $154,800 total"[4]

A savings of $97,920 over the life of the loan for just $158 more each month...AND YOU OWN THE HOME OUTRIGHT IN HALF THE TIME!

Sometimes a picture is worth a thousand words, or in this case, thousands of dollars. This is a no-brainer, Deuce. A 15-year mortgage is a much better value.

Finally, the buy and sell mentality is generally profitable for real estate agents and not the property owner. They get a commission off of every transaction. You may or may not see a profit on the sale of your home. It depends on economic conditions. The hope of increased property value each time you sell is risky business. Ask my friend in California about his property value. In this situation, I'll take a lesson from the typical American millionaire; it makes better sense to buy and hold than sell every few years. If it goes up in value when you're ready to sell, then you've made a good investment. If it doesn't, you at least have additional equity in the home to buffer the loss.

Deuce, let me summarize my thoughts on homeownership and offer the following advice. The decision to rent or buy a primary residence should be based on individual circumstances and not on hopeful profits. Economic conditions and home values are difficult to predict. However, most wealthy Americans typically buy and own their homes. If you decide to buy, don't stretch your finances by purchasing more than you need or can reasonably afford. Trophy homes look great but cost much. A 15-year loan can save you thousands of dollars in interest payments compared to a 30-year loan. A 15-year note also expedites the process of building equity. Lastly, employ a buy and hold strategy when purchasing a house. The typical middle-class millionaire doesn't jump from house to house every few years. He parks his money in a sound residential property and watches the investment grow in value over time.

Deuce, the last recommendation I have on this matter is what many in the financial industry will warn against. If you are going to buy a permanent residence, it is usually better to pay off the mortgage than spend your life making payments. Most experts believe mortgage debt is "good" debt. I don't. I adamantly believe that meaningful wealth acquisition occurs after a mortgage is paid off.

Here's the process. If you purchase a house on a 15-year loan and retire the note in a shorter timeframe, you will have extra money to invest. Once the house is "paid in full," the money used for monthly mortgage payments can be placed in other asset building tools...such as index mutual funds. This is the method of creating wealth that comes from homeownership I referred to earlier: *Own the house outright and invest the savings elsewhere.* Ask yourself this question: What would happen if you had an extra grand or more to invest each month? ANSWER: You would reduce the time it takes to reach the goal of financial independence, *significantly*. Think about it.

Well, my young grandson, it's time for the travelers to fire up the Mobile Marriott and head south on interstate 35. I hope we can arrive in San Antonio by early evening. We have a park reservation near the Riverwalk and Dolly's been craving Mexican food. We may spend a day or two at Sea World as well. I wonder how old Shamu the Killer Whale really is. I look forward to hearing from you, Deuce.

Your Loving Grandfather,
Hancock

CHAPTER 13

Chariots

Dear Deuce,

This morning, Dolly and I decided to take a short detour to College Station before heading to the Alamo City. We were watching the history channel late last night and became fascinated by a special presentation on our 41st President, George Herbert Walker Bush. We didn't realize the Presidential library was located on the west campus of Texas A&M University until watching the program. As we pulled out of Grapevine, we decided to make a pit stop in Aggieland for a tour of President Bush's bibliotheca.

As we entered the campus of Texas A&M University, I recalled many football games between the Aggies of A&M and Razorbacks of Arkansas. The rivalry always brings out a great crowd of supporters for both teams. Through the years, Dolly and I have attended many of these events with friends and family. I always enjoy jabbing the Aggie faithful when the Hogs bring home a victory. Listening to the A&M alumni clumsily stammer through their list of excuses is sweet delight. I'm chuckling now just thinking about it.

The Presidential library is located on ninety acres and situated on a plaza adjoining the Presidential Conference Center and the Texas A&M Academic Center. The museum is the primary archive for Mr. Bush's private and public life. Childhood memorabilia and collectibles from his military service are on display. A World War II Avenger Torpedo Bomber, similar to one Mr. Bush flew as a navy pilot, proudly adorns the exhibition hall's ceiling. Mr. Bush also served our country as a U.S. Congressman, Ambassador to the United Nations, and Director of the CIA before assisting as Vice President to Ronald Reagan then President of the United States. He is a man of many talents.

President Bush's legacy focuses on the liberation of Kuwait when the country was brutally attacked by the villainous Saddam Hussein. The Persian Gulf War was Mr. Bush's response to the delusive tyranny of the Iraqi dictator. Egregious acts of unprovoked aggression must always be met with firm resolve. Once again, the American soldier carried the mantle of liberty and freedom on foreign soil. Today, Kuwait is a free nation because of the heroes of the U.S. military. President Bush is also a hero in my book.

Deuce, last week we pondered *the house* which is the most expensive purchase you'll ever make. This week, let's look at the second most expensive item: *the automobile*. Ahhh. We Americans have a fascination with our cars, don't we? During the colonial days of our country, transportation was something we brushed, fed oats, and parked in the barn. Today, it's something we polish, feed petroleum, and park in the garage. Things have changed.

The American chariot has evolved immensely since the days of Henry Ford. In the early days, the choice of colors for your favorite ride was pretty limited, black. Nothing else. Why? Mr. Ford wanted his automobile to be affordable for the average citizen. More colors meant added expense. He preferred a no frills machine at a much lower cost. What have we got today? Every color, style, and option you can imagine. Vehicles also come in a wide range of prices. You get to decide what's right for you.

The modern chariot has become much more than basic transportation. For many, it symbolizes who they are and where they see themselves on the ladder of success. It must be of a certain value and brand that communicates prestige or success. It provides an inflated image of who they are, or maybe, who they want to be. What's the real difference between a Mercedes-Benz and a Chevrolet other than perception and price? Must people prove themselves successful by owning a carriage that widens the chasm of debt just because it looks good? Is the Mercedes hood ornament really worth the price? Why is image so important?

I, myself, can't imagine owning a vehicle without automatic transmission, a CD player, and air conditioning. It must have all the options I desire or I won't consider the purchase either. Why? Are we all spoiled by the affluence of society? I think so.

The typical American family owns at least two cars. Once upon a time, I had four in my driveway. OUCH! Why did I do it? Is it really such an indispensable utility? Did you know that in some countries, the automobile is not the primary source of transportation? The citizens of Sweden rely heavily upon the bicycle. The Swedes are also in much better physical condition than we Americans. Whatever the reasons, owning a car carries with it a magical mystique in the mind of the average American.

The first car I owned was a 1965 Mercury Comet my folks purchased for $580. I loved that car, my own set of wheels. It represented *freedom* to a 16-year old junior in high school. It also began a serious lesson on the relationship between money and machines. A lesson I've learned well. They aren't cheap and they break down...often.

Deuce, shortly after owning and caring for my first car, I made a decision that I would never fall in love with a piece of metal again. Cars are expensive to own and operate, and they never showed their appreciation to me when I cared for them. It's nothing more than a shiny piece of aluminum that manages to tap into my financial well-being. Therefore, I have no loyalty whatsoever to my vehicle.

Now, having said this, I must state that proper maintenance is a must. If you own a car, you should take good care of it. Not because you love it, but because it's such an expensive item to own. You'll want your car to last a long time, and you'll want it to be dependable. An ounce of prevention in the form of general maintenance goes a long way.

The decision to buy a car is one we all face at some point. What to buy and what price to pay is a difficult and time consuming issue. I'm going to provide a few guidelines I've used for all my auto purchases. This list of hints may save you a little money and time when the urge to own captures your thoughts or the car you currently have reaches the end of its days.

Why own a car? This is a question that many answer incorrectly. If you have a car for the "image" it represents, then you own a vehicle for the wrong reason. Image is nothing more than a tool that dealers use to increase the price. I own a vehicle for one reason: transportation. Now I won't pretend that style and options aren't important. They are, as long as a reasonable price accompanies the vehicle. Deuce, if you can suppress the desire for a prestigious chariot, you'll save yourself thousands of dollars. Trophy cars are like trophy homes: expensive. The cost to insure a luxury car is also extreme.

What should you buy? This is a personal decision that only you can decide. I have a close friend who says he'll only purchase Japanese products because they're so reliable. I don't disagree. My father has owned Toyotas for many years for this reason. I have another friend who says that German vehicles are engineering marvels and run smoother than any other vehicle on the market. Again, no disagreement from me. American carmakers have also made major strides in design and dependability over the past few decades. You see, Deuce, it's a matter of preference. My only advice would be to avoid luxury vehicles such as Mercedes-Benz, Rolls Royce, and BMW. Reason: lofty purchase price, maintenance expense, and hefty insurance premiums.

In the book *The Millionaire Next Door*, Stanley and Danko state that more than 57 percent of millionaires in the USA own American made vehicles.[1] The brand they prefer over all others is Ford. "The most popular models include the F-150 pickup and the Explorer sports utility vehicle."[2] Do millionaires know something we don't? My advice: Buy vehicles with a reputation for reliability and high trade-in value. If you can forego the desire for upgrades and high end options, then buy a good, inexpensive economy car. Whenever I buy any vehicle, I always remain sensitive to my personal financial security. Financial independence has a much higher priority in my life than the type of car I drive.

Deuce, I should mention that some occupations necessitate the need for a luxury ride. A friend of mine drives a Mercedes-Benz because he often chauffeurs clients who expect first-class treatment. Sometimes pampering those who provide corporate revenue with style and comfort is good business. In this case, owning a prestigious machine may be in order.

How much should you pay for a car? My answer to this question is very simple. The less you pay the better. For this reason, I rarely buy anything brand new. A low mileage pre-owned vehicle can usually be purchased for thousands less than a new car. Also, a brand new car will lose *significant* value the moment it rolls off the showroom floor. I personally look for vehicles that are a year or two old with less than fifteen thousand miles on the odometer. My rationale centers on price. I want as much as I can get for the money I spend. I haven't bought a brand new car in over twenty-five years. This is nothing more than responsible stewardship. Why throw money at a piece of iron?

Also, don't be afraid to negotiate price on any car. Most vehicles are listed much higher than they're worth. I have never bought a car for the asking price and neither should you. If you can't agree on a reasonable price, walk away from the deal. I once walked away from a truck purchase because the dealer wouldn't reduce the asking price by $200. Oh well. There are always other chariots for sale.

Should you lease or finance a vehicle? The simple answer is this: neither. If you can pay cash for a car, do it. Remember, debt is the enemy of wealth. Stay away from debt if at all possible. If you must finance a vehicle, always purchase and *never* lease a car. Leasing is a great deal for the dealer only, not you. When you lease a car, you agree to make a nominal down payment on the automobile and make monthly payments for a set time period. The problem is this: At the end of the leasing agreement you must give the vehicle back to the dealership. You don't get to keep the car. You paid a significant amount of money for several years but have nothing to show for it. Never lease a vehicle. Leasing is not a good deal.

If you must finance a car, try to avoid terms of 4 years or more. This will ensure less interest paid to the financier and you'll own the chariot sooner. It may not be worth very much, but it's still yours to keep. Buying is always better than leasing.

How can you guarantee you aren't buying a lemon? You can't. Purchasing a vehicle can be a roll of the dice. Buying a car always has an element of risk attached. However, you can reduce risk by letting a good mechanic inspect the vehicle before you buy. I have a friend that owns an auto repair shop. He gives me his opinion on every vehicle I consider for purchase. I trust his advice and it's always time well spent. I usually pay him a small amount for his time and opinion.

You can also request a *Car Fax* from the salesman if you're using a dealership or you can order one online if the seller gives you the VIN number. This is a good source of information on the service history of the vehicle you're considering. It's not perfect, but it's better than nothing. The more information you obtain, the more likely you are to make a good decision. Move slowly when buying a car and don't let emotion impair your judgment. We love God and people, Deuce, not machines.

Now let me summarize my thoughts on buying and owning the American chariot:

1. Always provide your vehicle regular maintenance so it will last a long time.

2. Avoid buying luxury cars if possible; utility is more important than image.

3. Always buy vehicles with a reputation for reliability and high trade-in value.

4. Never buy brand new. Choose a late model, low mileage vehicle and save thousands.

5. Never lease a car. Buying is always better than leasing.

6. Never pay the asking price for a car.

7. Never let car ownership affect the goal of reaching financial independence.

Well, my grandson, I hope these helpful hints are beneficial. Owning a car is an expensive proposition. Whether the purchase was a wise decision is, at best, a gamble. Henry Ford made this statement, "The best we can do is size up the chances, calculate the risks involved, estimate our ability to deal with them and make our plans with confidence."[3]

Dolly and I will move on to San Antonio late this afternoon. Let me know if you have any questions. I'm only a phone call away...

Your Loving Grandfather,
Hancock

CHAPTER 14

Debt

Dear Deuce,

Hello from the hallowed grounds of the Alamo in beautiful downtown San Antonio. Dolly and I have spent the day rediscovering the history of Texas and dining at her favorite Mexican food restaurant. We took a leisurely stroll through the gardens of the Riverwalk then climbed aboard a party barge and enjoyed a short tour through scenic San Antonio. Our launch master kept yelling at the passing tourist: "Welcome to *San Diego!*" His bellowing was met with furled brows and perplexed expressions. Could it be that he's a bit geographically challenged? Anyway, it was a great day that ended with our visit to the most popular tourist spot in Texas, the Alamo.

The Alamo was originally built around 1718 and named Mission San Antonio de Valero. The location was used for sheltering missionaries and Indian converts for nearly 70 years.

Toward the end of the century, Spanish officials residing on the property distributed the farmlands surrounding the Alamo to local Indian residents.

There are two explanations for how the term "Alamo" came to pass; both have elements of truth. The historical version suggests that Spanish soldiers occupying the structure in the early 1800's coined the term "Alamo." They called the mission "El Alamo" in honor of their hometown, Alamo de Parras, Coahuila. The botanical version for the mission's name centers on the Spanish word for "poplar tree" which is "Alamo." Cottonwood trees are a type of poplar that was at one time prominent in the area.

The battle between General Antonio Lopez de Santa Anna's army and the Texan defenders, led by William B. Travis began on February 23, 1836. It is believed the Mexican army outnumbered the Texans, 20 to 1. Jim Bowie, James Bonham, and Davy Crockett were among the heroes who resisted Santa Anna's army for almost 13 days before falling in defeat. The Mexican general was a ruthless man who took no prisoners when surrender was offered. The merciless massacre became a battle-cry for Texas' succession from Mexico. *Remember the Alamo!*

The Alamo is now viewed as a place where men struggled against impossible odds and gave the ultimate sacrifice for freedom. This is why the Alamo is considered the Shrine of Texas Liberty. We must never forget those whose blood was shed for freedom and liberty.

Deuce, there's a classic movie depicting the events of the Alamo that plays continuously at the IMAX theater close by. Dolly and I have made this trip several times over the years, and we always end our day with popcorn at the IMAX. The Alamo is a spectacular piece of Texas history and the IMAX show is worth the ticket.

Well, now that we've discussed the independence of Texas, time to move on to the matter of financial independence. The subject of the day is one that should have been discussed weeks ago: *debt!* I can sum up this whole lesson in one sentence: DEBT

IS THE ENEMY OF WEALTH. Have a great week, Deuce. Bye-bye...

No, no. There's more...but debt really is the enemy of wealth. Financial independence will never be attained unless one reconciles debt and the affect it has on net worth. Furthermore, debt is a noose around a person's neck that will squeeze the life out of any financial plan. Debt makes you a slave. Proverbs chapter 22, verse 7 says, "The rich rule over the poor, and the borrower is servant to the lender."[1] Do you want to be a slave for the rest of your life? Do you want to be hounded by debt collectors? Of course not.

Let me begin by challenging a few fairy tales about debt. There are those who will tell you there is something called "Good Debt" and "Bad Debt." They claim that Good Debt is investment debt that creates value such as a mortgage, student loan, or real estate loan. If you can get a loan that has a tax write-off, a low interest loan that may provide for future earnings potential, or a loan that increases wealth in the long run, then it would be considered good debt. I can't believe I actually wrote that down: a loan that increases wealth. What?? Talk about a paradox. *Debt does not increase wealth...ever. Debt makes you poor. PERIOD!* Deuce, there is no such thing as "Good Debt." It is all "Bad Debt." Anything that makes you a slave to a lender is bad debt. Refer back to Proverbs 22:7.

Now that I have this principle firmly entrenched in your flawless memory, I'm going to say something that will make you scratch your head and go "Huh??" Although the Bible warns against debt, it doesn't specifically prohibit debt. Therefore, I'm going to play a game of semantics. Here we go: I will concede to something called "Necessary Debt," not "Good Debt." I know I'm traveling down a slippery path, Deuce. I do so with a begrudging spirit. I'm kicking and screaming all the way. I hate the idea, but in a capitalist society like ours, we have to play the game of debt in a responsible manner. There are some things that we can only have if we acquire a loan. Dog gone it!

Most Americans could never own a house unless they take out a mortgage. This is necessary debt, not good debt. Some Americans would never reap the benefits of an advanced education unless they take out a school loan. This is necessary debt, not good debt. A business may not grow unless equipment or property is purchased with a business loan. This is necessary debt, not good debt. I'll even suggest that financing an automobile may be necessary debt. OUCH! That goes against my own convictions! What's important is this: If debt is incurred, it must be done in a responsible manner.

Are you scratching your head yet? I wouldn't blame you if you were. Let me pause and make this statement. If there is any way to avoid debt, then do so. In the book *The Richest Man in Babylon* by George S. Clason, the gold lender makes this observation about debt, "It is a pit of sorrow and regrets where the brightness of the sun is overcast and night is made unhappy by restless sleeping."[2] I don't need the pit of debt interrupting my sleep. Do you?

One of my favorite Christian authors, Dave Ramsey says, "...debt is an aggressive, fast-spreading, and financially deadly cancer."[3] I'm in complete agreement. However, you probably can't own a home without obtaining a mortgage. So what do you do? Be responsible.

Never take out a loan that you can't repay quickly. For a mortgage, use a 15-year loan, not a 30-year. Never buy a house for the maximum amount the lender says you can afford. No one needs that much house. The lender doesn't care about you or your finances. He wants to make money. If you're going to buy a car, don't buy a brand new $50,000 BMW and finance for 7 years. Think about buying a pre-owned Chevy with low miles for half the price and finance it for 3 years. A better idea would be to buy a late model Ford and pay cash! The point is this: If you must finance, be smart and responsible. Also, pay off the loan quickly. The longer you finance, the heavier the burden.

Any discussion about debt must include the credit card industry. Credit cards in American society have become big business over the years. I must get a half a dozen applications in the mail each week. Do you know why credit card companies flood us with junk mail? Here's why. The typical credit card-holder in America carries a balance of over $8000 from month to month. The average interest rate is 18.3%.[4] As you can see, this is a high profit business. They want us to have as many credit cards as we can stuff in our wallets. Why? 18.3% interest.

Deuce, it would be wise to avoid using credit cards completely. You may want to destroy them. Ramsey says if we have credit cards, we should all participate in "...a plastic surgery party."[5] Take a pair of Big Chief scissors and cut them up. *All of them!* This is a good idea. A "debit card," which is an extension of your checking account, can always be used in place of a credit card. Your checking account will be reduced at the moment you use the debit card, so it's like paying cash. Plus, there's no interest rate associated with a debit card. Debit cards are much better than credit cards.

Credit card debt is the easiest to obtain and most difficult to remove. Credit card debt can ruin relationships and paralyze a person's motivation. If you must use a credit card, pick a low interest card that does not require a membership fee and pay off the thing in full each month. Discipline yourself to be the master of debt. Don't let a credit card control your life.

The subject of your "credit score" is something that always comes up when discussing debt. This is an important number that is used to determine your credit "worthiness." Your credit worthiness will determine whether a company is willing to offer you a loan and the interest rate that company will charge. The better your "worthiness" or credit score, the lower your interest rate will be. "Worthiness" is another way of asking; *Are you responsible enough to pay your debt according to the terms of the loan?* The answer will be reflected in your credit score. The higher your credit score, the more responsible or "worthy" you are to repay your debt.

Deuce, I'm not going into the details of determining credit scores. It's a complex process and I'm not sure anyone fully understands the credit score formula. I will say this; always pay your bills on time and you will never have a problem obtaining a loan...anywhere. Do not max-out your credit cards and always pay them off each month...*in full!* Avoid debt and your credit score will always be in the excellent range.

Let me summarize my thoughts as follows:

1. Debt is the enemy of wealth.

2. There is no such thing as "Good Debt." Debt is always bad.

3. If you must finance, be smart and responsible.

4. Use a debit card and avoid using credit cards if at all possible.

5. If you must use a credit card, pay it off in full each month. Don't leave a balance.

6. Always remember, the borrower is a slave to the lender.

Deuce, debt is an ugly predator that speaks in poetic prose. When you see Mr. Jones wearing a Rolex watch, driving a shiny new Cadillac, and storing a bass boat and motorcycle in his garage, you may begin to experience feelings of envy. It is a temptation that's often difficult to resist. The sweet sound and lure of materialism can be a trap for the most disciplined among us. Debt can have a devastating affect on your financial progress if it isn't captured and managed with fierce conviction. You must beat it into submission. Over the past few years, the occurrence of bankruptcies, foreclosures, and bank failures has increased to epidemic proportions. Debt is the cause. I know I said this earlier, but it is important to remember: DEBT IS THE ENEMY OF WEALTH!

Well my young financial apprentice, we are rapidly approaching the end of your formal training. You'll be doing journeyman's work before you know it. The fundamental pieces of the American Dream have been presented. I'll have a few final thoughts to share in the coming weeks, but the foundation for wealth has been laid. I hope it's been beneficial.

Dolly and I will be leaving for California in the morning. The attack dachshund has been fed and the Mobile Marriott has been filled. I wonder if Davy Crockett ever climbed on a surfboard. I'm sharpening my Bowie knife, putting on my coonskin cap, and off to the left coast we go…

Your Loving Grandfather,
Hancock

CHAPTER 15

Spending

Dear Deuce,

Dolly and I have just completed a tour of the Ronald Reagan Library in Southern California. We were told the Presidential exhibition with thousands of artifacts and memorabilia is one of the most visited sites in the country. President Reagan is possibly the most meritorious and effective politician of my generation. The title, "The Great Communicator" is richly deserved.

As we entered the regal building memorializing Reagan's accomplishments, the Presidential aircraft he used is prominently displayed. Air Force One, a Boeing 707, appears to be in graceful ascension as it rests on reinforced pedestals. We also examined a piece of the Berlin Wall on the grounds near his final resting place. A replica of the Oval Office is available for view and adorned with personal belongings of Mr. Reagan.

Nancy Reagan has a special area in the library as well. Dolly marveled at the fashion gallery that exhibits many of Mrs. Reagan's formal dresses worn on special occasions. Together, the Reagans brought hope, dignity, and confidence back to the White House after the malaise of the Carter administration. His wit and humor and her class and gracefulness prompt fond memories.

Interestingly, the Executive Director of the library was one of my classmates in junior high while living in Oak Harbor, Washington. At first glance, I didn't recognize him. After a few minutes of casual conversation, we both realized our common history. It was good to see him.

Deuce, President Reagan was the guest speaker at a banquet for the National Rifle Association in 1983. As he addressed the audience, these words drew applause, "If we could just keep remembering that Moses brought down from the mountain the Ten Commandments, not ten suggestions - and if those of us who live for the Lord could remember that He wants us to love our Lord and our neighbor, then there's no limit to the problems we could solve or the mountains we could climb together as a mighty force."[1] Even in his element, the President understood the necessity of the sovereign influence of a righteous creator. Our current leaders could take a lesson from Ronald Reagan. God bless The Great Communicator.

Mr. Reagan assumed the Office of President in January of 1981. His inaugural address was one of hope and prosperity as American hostages in Iran were being released the same day. Our countrymen watched a brave and courageous visionary assume the mantle of world leader at a time when U.S. authority in international affairs was being challenged. He would face many trials during his administration with confidence and passion.

In August of 1981, President Reagan was confronted with a domestic matter that required strength and resolve. On August 3rd the nation's air traffic controllers union organized an illegal strike against the government. The leaders of the Professional Air Traffic Controller's Organization, PATCO, instructed its members to discontinue their work obligations in protest over economic matters. Nearly 14,000 controllers lost their jobs. This significant event in our country's history is where my story begins.

I was hired as a public servant of the United States in October of 1981 and began my career as an air traffic controller. I also had the privilege of meeting Christ for the first time about a month later. These two consecutive events changed my life in dramatic fashion. I would never be the same.

I was also fortunate to marry a very godly woman who recognized my spiritual shallowness and managed to get me involved in a Christian church in Albuquerque, New Mexico. Dolly's influence and prayers have sustained me through many moments of tribulation. She is my best friend.

As Dolly and I made our home in Albuquerque, several men on the church softball team provided me wisdom and counsel at a time when I was searching for answers. As I grew in Christ, God opened my eyes to things I'd never known. The scales were removed. Reading the Bible regularly and having a consistent prayer life is now something the old man doesn't neglect. God's Word is food for the soul.

In 1986, my wife of four years informed me that she was pregnant with twins. WHAT? I'M NOT READY! At that moment I realized my finances were in shambles and I'd better get prepared for fatherhood. At the ripe old age of 28, I began a sustained study of personal finance and wealth in America. Over the next several years, God showed me the meaning of money and how it relates to a Christian's life. What I discovered are the items we've discussed these past few weeks. I've passed them on to you because it's information I wish I'd known at your age. Unfortunately, no one gave me any formal training on the subjects. I had to learn them on my own. Hopefully, you won't let time linger before finding the truth about the American Dream. It's real and it's within reach. More importantly, I hope you'll accept Jesus as Lord and Savior if you haven't already.

There is one tectonic truth about wealth I haven't mentioned up to this point. Here it is: *It's not what you make that counts; it's what you keep.* Deuce, you've probably heard this maxim before and it seems like such an elementary premise. Even the simplest of minds can comprehend the idea. Still, the basics of wealth are often unintentionally neglected. Although a high salary is helpful in reaching financial independence, it isn't necessary. You don't have to make a million dollars to be a millionaire. What is paramount for success is living below your means, regardless of income, and SAVE, SAVE, SAVE. Let me give you a simple method for living below your income and a process for building wealth at an accelerated rate. These two techniques for wealth acquisition have literally made our retirement years carefree.

To be effective at living below your income, you must prioritize your spending. Prioritizing begins with a commitment to the spending principle of 30/70. This is a process of ensuring you live below your means. Here's how it works; prioritize your spending by earmarking your income this way:

1. Give ten percent to God (your local church.)

2. Place ten percent in retirement accounts (401(k)s and IRAs.)

3. Place ten percent in investment accounts (Index Mutual Funds.)

4. Live on the remaining 70 percent.

5. Never compromise on items one through four.

Deuce, the financial experts will tell you to pay yourself first. I say NO! *Pay God first and you second.* Remember, if you put God first in all you do, God will be on your side in all you do. Additionally, put items one through three on automatic withdrawal from your checking account. Have your bank transfer the funds from checking to the earmarked accounts each payday. Automatic investing will ensure you're consistent about saving and bulwark against the urge to compromise. It makes the process of building wealth something you don't have to think about. It just happens every payday, like clockwork. As you can see, you'll be investing 30 percent of your income before you ever pay a bill. Automating the process is vital to living below your means. *It's not what you make that counts; it's what you keep.*

Now, let me clarify what living below your means really is. It doesn't mean you hoard your money or live like a hermit. It doesn't mean you keep a white-knuckle grip on everything you make. It simply means living responsibly and spending in an intelligent manner. It means being a good steward of the assets God gives you. You can still go to a nice restaurant or movie on occasion. However, your commitment is to live on the remaining 70 percent of income through careful budgeting and adopting a frugal lifestyle. This will take self-discipline and willpower. You may feel the urge to forego your commitment. The impulse to spend is the sweet whisper of materialism. Deuce, draw a line in the sand and hold fast to your plan. Financial freedom is at hand.

The next technique dramatically accelerated the Hancock wealth acquisition plan. I mentioned in a previous correspondence that you should retire a home mortgage as quickly as possible. It can be done in a relatively painless manner; however, it requires assertiveness and determination.

As I stated previously, buy a house in a safe, middle-class neighborhood and pay it off quickly. Use only a 15-year mortgage when financing your home. Then commit to pay off the note completely in ten years. Your next question is: "How do you accomplish that?" ANSWER: Bi-weekly payments instead of monthly payments. This alone will remove nearly three years from a 15-year mortgage because you'll make an extra month of payments each year due to the bi-weekly payment schedule.

Deuce, typically mortgage lenders are willing to work with you on developing a plan to accelerate the payoff of your loan.

Shortly after purchasing my home, I called the lender and told him I wanted to own the house in ten years. We discussed the bi-weekly payment option at length. He then said if I included an additional amount every two weeks and applied the sum to principle only, I could pay off the loan, in full, within ten years. I leaped at the offer. By owning the house outright I have accelerated wealth creation exponentially! It works, Deuce! Once the house was paid in full, the money used for bi-weekly payments was then earmarked for additional investing. What an incredible difference it's made to our financial security.

Deuce, the two methods above combined with compound interest has streamlined the cause of financial freedom in the Hancock house. Financial security has a liberating affect on one's outlook on life. Remember, it is imperative that you prioritize your spending by putting God first, living below your means, owning your house, and never yielding your principles. Then watch God make the ordinary become extraordinary. You'll see financial freedom charging in your direction. You'll also witness opportunities to use your wealth for causes and events that honor God. There's one thing better than having wealth; it's giving it away.

Well, my grandson, questions may arise about prioritizing spending and living below your means. Give me a call or drop me a note. I'm always here for you. Reducing your income by 30 percent sounds more difficult than it really is. However, it is a critical principle on the road to financial freedom. We'll discuss the importance of freedom and other things that matter next week.

As we approach the final lessons on reaching the American Dream, I hope our discussions have been beneficial. Deuce, I'm encouraged by your commitment and eagerness to succeed. You're doing well.

Dolly and I have decided to take a Hawaiian cruise out of Los Angeles for the next two weeks. This should be a fun and relaxing time for both of us. I'm looking forward to feeling the warm trade winds of Waimea Bay. While we're gone, Reggie, the attack dachshund, is being cared for by a local pet hotel.

Can you believe there's something called a "pet hotel"? Why do I have a dog?

Your Loving Grandfather,
Hancock

CHAPTER 16

Myths

Dear Deuce,

Dolly and I are inside the Mobile Marriott and packing for our voyage to the Hawaiian Islands. We set sail tomorrow morning and we're looking forward to fair skies and calm waters. A tropical cruise is the best way to conclude our tour of U.S. historic sites. Tracing our country's history reinforces how blessed we are to live in America.

This morning we took a short excursion to the San Diego Aircraft Carrier Museum at Navy Pier in San Diego Bay. An old aircraft carrier called the U.S.S. Midway has been transformed into a floating museum for military history. It is a fascinating ship to explore with a unique chronicle of service to our country.

The U.S.S. Midway is one of the longest-serving aircraft carriers in the United States Navy. The warship was commissioned in 1945, shortly after World War II ended. It was named after a significant victory for the allied forces on Midway Island in the South Pacific. The ship carried a crew of 4500 men and served nearly 13,000 meals a day. It is the length of three football fields, which is a hundred feet longer than the Titanic. The warship was decommissioned in 1992 after 47 years of active duty. The number "41" painted on the side represents the order in which the carrier began honorable service for the country. The newest aircraft carrier in the American fleet is the U.S.S. George H.W. Bush bearing the number 77.

The harbor-bound museum houses vintage warplanes of our military and showcases pictures and videos of the carrier's active days around the world. We observed the boat's engine room, sleeping quarters, and hangar before having lunch in the galley. These old battleships have a heritage of preserving and protecting liberty. The veterans who served, and those serving today, are the real heroes of America. We must never allow the defense of our country to be weakened or jeopardized.

Deuce, for the dialogue today I'm going to swerve into an area that's been troubling me for some time. The culture in which we live has created a few myths about wealth that I hope to dispel. On the issues of success and affluence, the "thought police" of our society can persuade the most seasoned freethinker to believe his values are naïve or unjust. Political correctness is a nefarious attempt to distort the truth.

Political correctness is a dangerous tool if not exposed for what it is: a restriction of free speech. In my opinion, political correctness is for those who are too weak to stand up for what's right. It permits angry people to hide their true beliefs behind the shield of shallow thought. Allow me to debunk a few of the wealth myths currently trumpeted by the politically correct crowd.

On any given day, the American media will attack wealthy citizens with a barrage of unfounded accusations. The anti-rich climate in our society is also perpetuated by politicians toting fairness for all at the expense of a few. *"Let's tax the rich!"* has become a common political mantra. The idea of possessing wealth has almost become an anti-American tenet in the eyes of the politically correct. Our media and politicians have vilified successful people and made outrageous critique of their abundance a sporting event. Ridiculing those who've managed opportunities for acquiring wealth is now common practice. What's happened to our country? Isn't life, liberty, and the pursuit of happiness a genuinely patriotic path for our citizens? Why does anyone look down upon a person of means? Don't we all desire affluence? I'm curious: When was the last time a poor person offered someone a job?

Class warfare and wealth-bashing are not American principles. They've been encouraged by mean-spirited elitists who want successful people to feel guilty about their reward. I recently heard an American President say he wants to redistribute wealth in our country. He implied that "life's lottery" favors only a few and opportunities for wealth are not available to everyone. Therefore, we must take from the rich who've earned their fortunes, and give it to those who haven't. His statements insinuate a "punish success" mentality. Does it seem right that a government official would suggest that we take the assets of any American, wealthy or not, and give them to someone else? Sounds like tyranny in action to me.

When I finished reading *The Millionaire Next Door* several years ago, I had to wonder why a millionaire would want to live in a middle-class neighborhood. Is it possible that wealthy people have had enough of the politically correct agenda and wish to remain anonymous? Why does so much criticism exist for wealthy Americans? Don't we all want financial independence? Don't we all want self-sufficiency? Isn't this what the Founding Fathers were eloquently proclaiming in the Declaration of Independence? So what happened to our country that made citizens turn against each other? Why do media elitists resent those who are making the American Dream a reality?

Wealthy Americans are not members of some evil empire. They are citizens of a country where opportunity exists for everyone, and they took advantage of those opportunities.

Opportunities are usually made, not given by life's lottery. Making your own way is an American ideal. America is where wealth is created, so why marginalize those who do? Affluent people are also job creators. They own businesses that provide others in society a way to support their families. Is it wise to bite the hands that feed us?

Did you know the number of requests for American citizenship from foreigners is at record levels? Deuce, it's the opportunity to achieve that draws people from around the world to the USA. Nowhere else is wealth available to so many. Wealthy citizens are people who've acquired life, liberty, and happiness through hard work. They're Americans.

Now I realize there are some who've received their wealth through inheritance. The Kennedys, Heinzes, and Rockefellers have passed their fortunes on to family members for several generations. However, this group composes a very small percentage of wealthy Americans and does not represent the majority.

Let's look at a few myths about wealthy citizens and counter the falsehoods with facts. For this exercise in myth-busting, I'll refer to information found in The Millionaire Next Door, the Public Affairs Office of the Department of the Treasury, and the New York Times. I have found no one who disputes these truths.

Myth: Rich people don't deserve their wealth. I suppose there may be some who believe that hard work isn't deserving of wealth. I'm not one. The truth is this: About 80 percent of the millionaires in this country are first generation affluent.[1] This means they achieved wealth on their own. They earned it. It wasn't given to them by way of inheritance. They started businesses, took risks, invested their capital, and saved. They became wealthy the American way.

Myth: Rich people don't have real jobs. Where in the world does this idea come from? Nearly two-thirds of all millionaires in this country work between forty-five and fifty-five hours each week. Although wealthy Americans typically own small businesses, the businesses they own could be described as "dull-normal." Typical vocations for the average millionaire include welding-contractors, auctioneers, rice farmers, mobile-home park owners, pest controllers, and paving contractors.[2] Aren't these real jobs?

Myth: Rich people don't pay their fair share of individual income taxes. According to the Department of the Treasury, wealthy Americans account for the majority of tax revenue received. A recent treasury department publication revealed: "...the top 5 percent of taxpayers paid more than one-half (53.8 percent) of all individual income taxes..."[3] The top 25 percent of taxpayers paid over 80 percent. Interestingly, "Taxpayers who rank in the top 50 percent of taxpayers by income pay virtually all income taxes."[4] Does this sound like wealthy citizens are doing something fraudulent or are they paying their fair share of American taxes? The truth will set us free.

Myth: Rich people hoard their money. A recent article in the New York Times stated more than 98 percent of the nation's richest households give to charities. "Those in the top 3.1 percent are responsible for 60 to 75 percent of the $360 billion given to charitable work..."[5] The New York Times is not a newspaper that's overly friendly toward wealthy Americans. Yet, this article is a testimony to the attitude affluent Americans have about philanthropy. Does this sound like the rich are hoarding their wealth? Where does this mendacious nonsense come from?

Deuce, I bring up this issue as a warning against the deception of political correctness. The vitriol toward wealthy citizens is usually without merit. You can't always believe the things you hear from those who disapprove of the affluent. Acquiring wealth for the right reasons is not un-American: quite the opposite. Abraham Lincoln said, "That some achieve great success, is proof to all that others can achieve it as well."[6] Our Founding Fathers wanted a country where wealth was within reach of every American. However, wealth-bashing is alive and well in our society. Class warfare is the first step to socialism, and I fear we're well on the way.

Remember this, my grandson: Wealth is freedom and freedom is what makes America the greatest country on earth. Don't let anyone lay a guilt trip on you for planning to succeed. Financial independence is a worthy cause. Therefore, "Go confidently in the direction of your dreams! Live the life you've imagined."[7]

Your Loving Grandfather,
Hancock

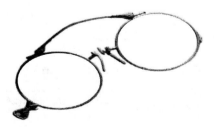

CHAPTER 17

Success

Dear Deuce,

Greetings from the 50th state and island paradise called Hawaii. Dolly and I have had an eventful day in the capital city of Honolulu. Feeling the warm surf and watching the tropical blue skies have generated many fond memories of my youth. I'm sporting this incredibly hideous Polynesian shirt that looks like an old, wilted Mother's Day arrangement. Why am I wearing this silly thing! Still, Hawaii is a special place that every American should visit in their lifetime.

This is the first port of call the ship will make on our scenic cruise through the Hawaiian Islands. We departed Los Angeles and spent five exceptional days on the smooth Pacific Ocean. Our stateroom came equipped with a balcony for evening relaxation. The food, service, and entertainment have exceeded my expectations. We may take up residence on this little boat.

Yesterday, Dolly and I toured the west side of Oahu, one of eight islands that form the Aloha State. Oahu is the most populated island of the Hawaiian chain and remains a well traveled tourist destination. The volcanic mountain also serves as a strategic military location in the South Pacific.

Deuce, as a teenager, my family lived on Oahu for a short time because of my father. Your great grandfather was a Chief Petty Officer in the United States Navy and made a full career of military service. His commitment and dedication to our country was honorable and deserving of our praise. His active duty years included the conflicts of the Korean and Viet Nam wars. I'm very proud to have a father who served in the armed forces of the United States. Patriotism is a Hancock family trait.

Dad was stationed at a military base on the west side of Pearl Harbor. Before activating his retirement request, our family spent nearly three years at Barber's Point Naval Air Station. I have explicit memories of carrying my surfboard to a nearby beach with several of my buddies. It was an experience I've recalled many times over the years. Dolly and I traveled to the duplex the Hancocks occupied at Iroquois Point and visited the school I attended, James Campbell High. My youthful days on Oahu have special meaning though things have changed profoundly.

This morning we hopped aboard an aqua shuttle and visited the Arizona Memorial in Pearl Harbor. On December 7, 1941, Japanese forces attacked our military bases on Oahu. The unprovoked onslaught resulted with the sinking of the battleship U.S.S. Arizona and the loss of over 1100 American sailors onboard. Until then, President Franklin D. Roosevelt resisted U.S. entry into World War II. However, this event changed the course of history. The Arizona Memorial serves as a reminder that tyranny and aggression can happen at any moment and won't be tolerated. The American soldier is the reason we still live in a free society.

Interestingly, the U.S.S. Missouri is docked nearby and can be seen from the floating shrine. The warship is the site where axis leaders of the Japanese military surrendered to the United

States, thereby ending World War II. This is uniquely significant; the place where the war began and ended for America is only a few yards apart.

Well, my grandson, your question regarding the spending principle of 30/70 is not only valid but deserving of explanation. At first glance, apportioning ten percent of your income to the local church may appear to be a "gift" and not an "investment." However, it's been my experience that whenever I give first to God, the blessings I receive in return are significantly bountiful. I believe that God has not only protected our family from unexpected tribulation, but also increased our wealth because of the commitment to give to Him the first fruits of our labor. When the windows of heaven are open, God can make your barns overflow.

Now, don't misunderstand my position. I don't believe that giving ten percent to God will "guarantee" wealth, health, or an easy life. It doesn't. I give for two reasons: obedience and a desire to show respect for Him who owns it all. It makes no sense to me that I should shortchange God since He is why I exist in the first place. Everything I have belongs to Him. I'm just a temporary manager of God's possessions. Giving ten percent to God has always been the first and best investment to make. I'm certain there are many who will challenge my position. That's okay. Spiritual matters don't always make sense to the unspiritual. For me, giving to God is the perfect investment. Let's move on.

Deuce, as we come to the end of my advice on financial security, I feel compelled to explain my thoughts on success and how one knows if success has been achieved. We've discussed practical steps for acquiring wealth and preparing your mind to reach affluence. Wealth and happiness are not always in unison nor are wealth and success. Success should never be defined by the size of your bank account or the value of your assets. Life is much more than money and possessions. Jesus said, "Watch out! Be on your guard against all kinds of greed; a man's life does not consist in the abundance of his possessions."[1]

Now I'm not going to pretend that wealth isn't an important commodity on the mortal side of heaven. It is, but the reason has little to do with money and more to do with relationships. Through the years, I've discovered the definition of success to be a personal issue that evolves with time.

During my young adult years when poverty was a whisper away, possessions and money were in high demand. If you don't have anything of value, you want everything. Therefore, my view of success was somewhat skewed. My callow vision of successful living had dollar signs attached. This is not a healthy perspective. As my salary increased and my belongings grew, the desire to acquire more diminished. I wonder why. It may have something to do with finding real purpose in life instead of collecting trinkets and tokens.

Deuce, this may sound like a philosophical definition of success, but it's one that fits all ages: Success is being in the center of God's will each day. A sense of peace engulfs my day when I put God first and yield to His control. Striving for His presence on a daily basis has produced blessings beyond explanation. Peace and success are inseparably bound when God controls your life.

I have found that wealth yields a product that should never be taken for granted: freedom. Freedom is what makes our country the greatest in the world. Freedom is what motivates people to achieve more than they are otherwise capable. Freedom provides options. Ronald Reagan said, "...freedom is not the sole prerogative of a chosen few, but the universal right of all God's children."[2] Financial freedom allows you to do something substantial for God's people. There's only one thing better than obtaining wealth; it's giving it away.

When a person of God uses his wealth for God's purposes, the return is much greater than the gift. God often allows you to see the difference your wealth has made in someone's life. This generates purpose for living. You become God's ambassador. Can you think of a better reason to have financial security?

Through the years, Dolly and I have supported missionaries at home and abroad. We've helped underprivileged people with financial assistance and supported church projects of all kinds. I don't mention this with haughty pride. I share this with extreme humility. It was done because God blessed the Hancocks abundantly, not because of us. Touching lives for God is what He wants us to do. II Corinthians, chapter 9, verse 9 says, "...The godly man gives generously to the poor. His good deeds will be an honor to him forever."[3] I'm thankful for the opportunity to give. The ability to give makes wealth meaningful.

Several years ago I came across an interesting discourse by James Dobson. His words are vividly etched in my memory: "I have concluded that the accumulation of wealth, even if I could achieve it, is an insufficient reason for living. When I reach the end of my days, a moment or two from now, I must look backward on something more meaningful than the pursuit of houses and land and machines and stocks and bonds. Nor is fame of any lasting benefit. I will consider my earthly existence to have been wasted unless I can recall a loving family, a consistent investment in the lives of people, and an earnest attempt to serve the God who made me. Nothing else makes much sense."[4] Dr. Dobson understands the value of relationships and the true meaning of wealth. This may be the finest definition of success I've ever read.

As our day in paradise comes to an end, Dolly and I are sitting at an oceanside grill overlooking Wiamea Bay along the north shore of Oahu. Surfers are enjoying the late afternoon swells of the Bonzai Pipeline. A warm and mild breeze wafts across the coconut trees. The smell of tanning oil hangs noticeably in the shoreline trade winds. A tiny umbrella is perched on my glass of Ginger Ale. We're casually devouring a bowl of boiled shrimp and a side order of manapua as we reflect on life and the meaning of success.

Deuce, we're thankful for many things. We're thankful for the blessing of living in a country where freedom and liberty are held in high esteem. We're thankful for a loving family and the relationships we have with our kids and grandkids. We're thankful for you, Deuce. We're thankful for friends that we care about and how they care for us. We're thankful that we can count more blessings than regrets. We're thankful for a God that has been with us every step of the way. We're thankful that we can give freely to God's people. We're thankful for the ability to serve Him.

Deuce, as Dolly and I enter the sunset of this existence, we recognize that God has allowed us to experience success beyond what we deserve. Success cannot be achieved without the blessings of the omnipresent Christ. Anything one perceives as success without God's oversight and approval is artificial. Success without God typically results in a false sense of accomplishment and probably won't last. Success without God is meaningless. God is the key ingredient in any success formula.

If I was to sum up the meaning of success at this point in my long and fulfilling life, it would encompass these four elements: faith, family, friends, and freedom. If you have these things in your life, you're successful. These are the things that matter…

Bless you my grandson,
Hancock

Glossary

1. **abeyance** - noun: temporary inactivity: suspension.

2. **aggrandized** - verb: to make appear great or greater: praise highly.

3. **altruistic** - adjective: unselfish regard for or devotion to the welfare of others.

4. **aphorism** - noun: a concise statement of principle.

5. **apposite** - adjective: highly pertinent or appropriate: apt.

6. **apropos** - adverb: with regard to the present topic: germane, fitting, or relevant.

7. **assuage** - verb: to lessen the intensity of (something that pains or distresses): ease: to put an end to by satisfying: appease, quench, or soothe.

8. **bastion** - noun: a fortified area or position: a stronghold or fortress.

9. **bibliotheca** - noun: a collection of books: library.

10. **bulwark** - noun: a strong support, a protective barrier: a rampart or shield.

11. **callow** - adjective: lacking adult sophistication: immature or naive.

12. **capsulate** - verb: to enclose in a capsule: summarize or finalize.

13. **cenotaph** - noun: a tomb or monument erected in honor of someone whose remains are elsewhere.

14. **didactic** - adjective: intending to teach, conveying information: instructional.

15. **egregious** - adjective: conspicuously bad: flagrant.

16. **fallacious** - adjective: deceptive or misleading, containing a fallacy: false.

17. **fetter** - noun: something that confines, restricts, or restrains.

18. **fruition** - noun: attainment of anything desired, realization of good results.

19. **grok** - verb: to understand profoundly and intuitively, to clearly comprehend.

20. **guileful** - adjective: deceitful and cunning.

21. **junto** - noun: a group of persons joined for a common purpose.

22. **malaise** - noun: an indefinite feeling of debility or lack of health often indicative of or accompanying the onset of an illness: sickly.

23. **mantra** - noun: a word or formula to be recited or sung.

24. **mendacious** - adjective: characterized by deception or falsehood.

25. **nefarious** - adjective: flagrantly wicked or evil: unethical.

26. **pabulum** - noun - intellectual sustenance, food for the mind, challenging ideas.

27. **paradox** - noun: a contradictory statement or having contradictory qualities.

28. **polemics** - noun: an aggressive attack on the opinions or principles of another.

29. **political correctness** - noun: a condition or state of being produced when: 1. one abandons their principles and beliefs to appease others, 2. one conforms to the wishes of a few without

regard for what's right and honorable, 3. one appears to be sensitive to a cause at the expense of truth, 4. one remains silent when action is appropriate: a false sense of doing what's right: weak-mindedness.

30. **philanthropy** - noun: an act or gift done or made for humanitarian purposes.

31. **sage** - noun: a person characterized by having wisdom and good judgment.

32. **tectonic** - adjective: having strong and widespread impact: meaningful, significant.

33. **tenets** - noun: beliefs, principles, or doctrines generally held to be true.

34. **vitriol** - noun: something highly caustic or severe in effect, as criticism: scathing.

35. **vox populi** - noun: popular sentiment, voice of the people, will of the majority.

36. **wafts** - verb: to move or go lightly by as if by impulse.

37. **zephyr** - noun: a gentle, light breeze from the west.

Notes

Every effort has been made to give complete bibliographic information for all references, quotes, and data. If the reader desires more specific information regarding any source, he or she should refer to the website and/or contact the author.

Preface

1. Paul J. Lim with George Mannes, "Money," cover story, *"How to Reach $1 Million,"* April 2011, Volume 40, Number 3, p. 61.

2. Franklin Quotes, *The Electric Ben Franklin,* Copyright 1999-2010, Independence Hall Association, Philadelphia, Pennsylvania, http://www.ushistory.org/franklin/quotable/singlrhtml. htm, (January 14, 2011).

Chapter 1: The Request

1. *"...give thanks in all circumstances, for this is God's will for you in Christ Jesus."* I Thessalonians 5:18 (NIV).

2. Theodore Roosevelt Quotes, Copyright 2010 BrainyMedia.com, *BrainyQuote,* http://brainyquote.com/quotes/authors/t/theodore_roos evelt_4.html, (January 14, 2011).

Chapter 2: Plan

1. Benjamin Franklin Quotes, Copyright 2010 BrainyMedia.com, *BrainyQuote,* http://brainyquote.com/quotes/authors/b/benjamin_fra nklin_9.html, (October 14, 2010).

2. Benjamin Franklin Quotes, Copyright 2010 BrainyMedia.com, *BrainyQuote*, http://brainyquote.com/quotes/authors/b/benjamin_fra nklin_2.html, (October 14, 2010).

3. Benjamin Franklin Quotes, Copyright 2010 BrainyMedia.com, *BrainyQuote*, http://brainyquote.com/quotes/authors/b/benjamin_fra nklin_2.html, (October 14, 2010).

4. *"Steady plodding brings prosperity, hasty speculation brings poverty."* Proverbs 21:5, (Living).

5. *"For I know the plans I have for you, declares the Lord, plans to prosper you and not harm you, plans to give you hope and a future."* Jeremiah 29:11, (NIV).

Chapter 3: Income

1. Thomas J. Stanley, Ph.D. and William D. Danko, Ph.D., *The Millionaire Next Door*, (New York: Pocket Books, 1998), p. 8.

2. Thomas J. Stanley, Ph.D. and William D. Danko, Ph.D., *The Millionaire Next Door*, (New York: Pocket Books, 1998), p. 9.

3. Benjamin Franklin Quotes, Copyright 2010 BrainyMedia.com, *BrainyQuote*, http://brainyquote.com/quotes/authors/b/benjamin_fra nklin_3.html, (January 14, 2011).

Chapter 4: The Gospel of Wealth

1. *"For the love of money is a root of all kinds of evil…"* I Timothy 6:10, (NIV).

2. *"For my determined purpose is that I may know Him…"* Philippians 3:10, (Amplified).

3. Gale Sayers and Al Silverman, *I Am Third*, (New York: Penguin Books, 2001), p. 42.

4. *"Better be poor and honest than rich and dishonest."* Proverbs 19:1, (Living).

Chapter 5: Retirement
1. George Foreman Quotes, Copyright 2010 BrainyMedia.com, *BrainyQuote*, http://www.brainyquote.com/quotes/authors/g/george_foreman.html, (October 13, 2010).

2. Benjamin Franklin Quotes, Copyright 2010 BrainyMedia.com, *BrainyQuote*, http://brainyquote.com/quotes/authors/b/benjamin_franklin_9.html, (January 14, 2011).

3. John C. Bogle, *The Little Book of Common Sense Investing: The Only Way to Guarantee Your Fair Share of Stock Market Returns*, (Hoboken: John Wiley and Sons, Inc., 2007), p. 205.

Chapter 6: Health Insurance
1. Benjamin Franklin Quotes, Copyright 2010 BrainyMedia.com, *BrainyQuote*, http://brainyquote.com/quotes/authors/b/benjamin_franklin_6.html, (January 14, 2011).

2. Benjamin Franklin Quotes, Copyright 2010 BrainyMedia.com, *BrainyQuote*, http://brainyquote.com/quotes/authors/b/benjamin_franklin_10.html, (January 14, 2011).

Chapter 7: Life Insurance
1. Benjamin Franklin Quotes, Copyright 2010 BrainyMedia.com, *BrainyQuote*, http://brainyquote.com/quotes/authors/b/benjamin_franklin_5.html, (January 14, 2011).

Chapter 8: Emergency Fund
1. Art Williams, "Common Sense: A Simple Plan for Financial Independence (Revised Edition)," (Doraville: Parkland Publishers, Inc., n.d.), p. 21.
Purdue University News, Office of Public Information, Purdue University (West Lafayete, IN), January 15, 1985, p.1.

2. Dave Ramsey, *Financial Peace Revisited*, (New York: Viking Penguin, 2003), p. 111.

Chapter 9: Individual Retirement Accounts
1. George W. Bush, Address on Initial Operations in Afghanistan, October 7, 2001, American Rhetoric, Copyright 2001-2009, (public domain), (October 18, 2010). http://www.americanrhetoric.com/speeches/gwbush911i nitialafghanistanops.htm

2. CCH Internet Research Network, News and Information, Pension-10/20/10, http://hr.cch.com/news/pension/102010a.asp, (October 22, 2010).
Employee Benefits Research Institute (EBRI), EBRI Press Release, PR#889, September 21, 2010.

Chapter 10: Investments
1. Henry David Thoreau Quotes, Copyright 2010 BrainyMedia.com, *BrainyQuote*, http://brainyquote.com/quotes/authors/h/henry_david _thoreau_7.html, (January 14, 2011).

2. Franklin Quotes, *The Electric Ben Franklin*, Copyright 1999-2010, Independence Hall Association, Philadelphia, Pennsylvania, http://www.ushistory.org/franklin/quotable/singlrhtml. htm, (January 14, 2011).

3. *"Work brings profit; talk brings poverty!"* Proverbs 14:23 (Living).

4. Patrick Henry Quotes, Copyright 2010 BrainyMedia.com, *BrainyQuote*, http://brainyquote.com/quotes/authors/p/patrick_henr y.html, (January 14, 2011).

5. Statue of Liberty Facts, Acceptance Statement by Grover Cleveland, 1886, http://www.endex.com/gf/buildings/liberty/liberty-facts.htm, (October 18, 2010).

6. John C. Bogle, *The Little Book of Common Sense Investing: The Only Way to Guarantee Your Fair Share of Stock Market Returns*, (Hoboken: John Wiley and Sons, Inc., 2007), p. 205.

7. Trends in Mutual Fund Investing, Investment Company Institute, August, 2010, http://www.ici.org/research/stats/trends/trends_08_10

Chapter 11: Compound Interest

1. *"Steady plodding brings prosperity..."* Proverbs 21:5, (Living).

2. Abraham Lincoln Quotes, Copyright 2010 BrainyMedia.com, *BrainyQuote*, http://brainyquote.com/quotes/authors/a/abraham_linc oln.html, (January 14, 2011).

3. John C. Bogle, *The Little Book of Common Sense Investing: The Only Way to Guarantee Your Fair Share of Stock Market Returns*, (Hoboken: John Wiley and Sons, Inc., 2007), p. 86.

4. Merriam-Webster, *Compound Interest*, http://www.merriam-eebster.com/dictionary/compound +interest?show=0&t=1299673611, (March 9, 2011).

5. Dave Ramsey, *Financial Peace Revisited*, (New York: Viking Penguin, 2003), chart, p. 120.

Chapter 12: Shelter
1. John F. Kennedy, *QuoteDB*, http://www.quotedb.com/quotes/2668, (January 14, 2011).

2. Thomas J. Stanley, Ph.D. and William D. Danko, Ph.D., *The Millionaire Next Door*, (New York: Pocket Books, 1998), p. 9.

3. Thomas J. Stanley, Ph.D. and William D. Danko, Ph.D., *The Millionaire Next Door*, (New York: Pocket Books, 1998), p. 9.

4. Dave Ramsey, *Financial Peace Revisited*, (New York: Viking Penguin, 2003), p. 89.

Chapter 13: Chariots
1. Thomas J. Stanley, Ph.D. and William D. Danko, Ph.D., *The Millionaire Next Door*, (New York: Pocket Books, 1998), p. 115.

2. Thomas J. Stanley, Ph.D. and William D. Danko, Ph.D., *The Millionaire Next Door*, (New York: Pocket Books, 1998), p. 115.

3. Henry Ford, *Best Quotes Poems*, Chance Sayings & Quotations, http://best-quotes-poems.com/chance-quotes.html, (January 14, 2011).

Chapter 14: Debt
1. *"The rich rule over the poor, and the borrower is servant to the lender."* Proverbs 22:7 (NIV).

2. George S. Clason, *The Richest Man in Babylon*, (New York, Signet Penguin, 1988), p. 83.

3. Dave Ramsey, *Financial Peace Revisited*, (New York: Viking Penguin, 2003), p. 70.

4. Dave Ramsey, *Financial Peace Revisited*, (New York: Viking Penguin, 2003), p. 74.

5. Dave Ramsey, *Financial Peace Revisited*, (New York: Viking Penguin, 2003), p. 78.

Chapter 15: Spending
1. The Ronald Reagan Foundation, Remarks at the Annual Members of The National Rifle Association, May 6, 1983 (public domain), (October 27, 2010). http://www.reaganfoundation.org/foundation-overview.aspx

Chapter 16: Myths
1. Thomas J. Stanley, Ph.D. and William D. Danko, Ph.D., *The Millionaire Next Door*, (New York: Pocket Books, 1998), p. 9.

2. Thomas J. Stanley, Ph.D. and William D. Danko, Ph.D., *The Millionaire Next Door*, (New York: Pocket Books, 1998), pages 9,10.

3. Department of the Treasury, Office of Public Affairs, Fact Sheet: *Who Pays the Most Individual Income Taxes?*, March 2, 2005.

4. Department of the Treasury, Office of Public Affairs, Fact Sheet: *Who Pays the Most Individual Income Taxes?*, March 2, 2005.

5. Jan M. Rosen, "The Rich Are Different From You and Me. They Give More," *The New York Times - Reprints* (November 10, 2010), http://www.nytimes.com/2010/11/11/giving/11CHOIC E.html?_r=2&pagewanted=print

6. Abraham Lincoln Quotes, Copyright 2010 BrainyMedia.com, *BrainyQuote*, http://brainyquote.com/quotes/authors/a/abraham_linc oln_5.html, (January 14, 2011)

7. The Quotations Page, Copyright 1994-2010, Henry David Thoreau, http://www.quotationspage.com/quote/27110.html, (November 18, 2010).

Chapter 17: Success

1. *"Watch out! Be on your guard against all kinds of greed; a man's life does not consist in the abundance of his possessions."* Luke 12:15. (NIV).

2. Ronald Reagan, Address to the 40th Session of the United Nations General Assembly in New York, New York, October 24, 1985, (public domain), (October 20, 2010).

3. *"...The godly man gives generously to the poor. His good deeds will be an honor to him forever."* II Corinthians 9:9. (Living).

4. James Dobson, *What Wives Wish Their Husbands Knew About Women*, (Carol Stream: Tyndale House Publishers, 2003), p. 108.

Themes

1. You don't have to make a million dollars to be a millionaire.

2. Success begins with a plan.

3. Work is the beginning of wealth.

4. Wealth and happiness are not always in perfect harmony.

5. Over time, small money becomes big money.

6. Life and accidents happen.

7. Hope for the best but plan for the worst.

8. Protect yourself from unexpected disasters.

9. Invest for the future with an Individual Retirement Account.

10. Own stocks through Index Mutual Funds.

11. Capture the magic of compound interest.

12. Save thousands with a 15-year mortgage.

13. Buying an auto is better than leasing.

14. Debt is the enemy of wealth.

15. Live below your means.

16. The myths are not supported with facts.

17. Success is being in the center of God's will each day.

About the Author

Gene Hutchins has been an air traffic controller for nearly 30 years. He is a husband, father, and devoted follower of Jesus Christ. He and his family currently reside in Grapevine, Texas where most of his time is spent serving his church and community. He occasionally likes to read and partake in fine dining at local restaurants. He also enjoys sporting events, attending concerts with friends, pretending to be a golfer, and watching a good movie.

Mr. Hutchins is a loyal fan of the Arkansas Razorbacks, Texas Rangers, and Dallas Mavericks. Although he's never owned an RV, he once drove his father-in-law's rig into a ditch near Greers Ferry, Arkansas. His father-in-law laughed hysterically!

Gene and Robin Hutchins   a.k.a. Hancock and Dolly

Reggie, The Attack Dachshund
Photo courtesy of Bill Glenn

The advice found in this book is divinely inspired, life experienced, and self-taught. His hope is that this book provides meaningful information on the basics of wealth and brings honor to God.

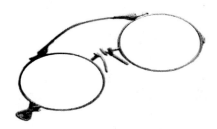

PERSONAL NOTES:

PERSONAL NOTES :

PERSONAL NOTES :